D1758800

ABOUT THIS BOOK

At the beginning of the seventeenth century, when European cities like London and Paris had long since risen to world fame, New York was still an unknown Indian village. It was not until the late eighteenth century that the former Nieuw Amsterdam grew into an important economic and financial center. It was at that time, too, that the city became a gathering place for the many immigrants who had left Europe as a result of economic misery or political pressure with hopes of starting a new life in America. New York stood for the unbroken optimism that inspired rich and poor alike – even if many immigrants were forced to eke out an existence in inhuman conditions in the Lower East Side. New York has had to suffer countless setbacks throughout its history, but even in its most difficult times the city could always count on the unbroken energy and pioneering spirit of its inhabitants. The

"Nine Eleven" terrorist attack was seen as an attack on the American soul, on the identity of an entire nation which on 4 July 1776 had proclaimed in the Declaration of Independence the pursuit of happiness to be an inalienable human right. And yet, the horror of these events and the pain caused by their memory brought forth during this time the willingness to help and the determination to persevere – and ultimately the unbroken optimism of the citizens of New York. Now, everyone would like to return to a normality that has in fact never existed in New York. And that is why the "Freedom Tower" is now called simply "1 World Trade Center", after its location. And it is fitting, too, that Times Square, long since "cleaned up", has been turned into a pedestrian area. New York is always changing – and always fascinating.

The view over the sea of houses of Midtown Manhattan at night, with its apparently never-ending sea of lights, shows us a world as it can be seen nowhere else in the world, a city full of energy and enthusiasm, full of hopes and longings, the stuff of dreams and yet absolutely real. In two words: New York.

TABLE OF CONTENTS

Above: As it grew dark we bought ourselves a small piece of pecan pie and sat down on a bench to watch the strings of lights between the towers over the river. The wind was whipping up white foam on the cold water, singing through the harp-like bridge and blowing screaming gulls around at will.   (Truman Capote)

Previous pages:
P. 1 The Statue of Liberty on Liberty Island
P. 2/3 »In a New York minute / Everything can change« (Don Henley)
P. 4/5 Times Square as a pedestrian zone
P. 6/7 The city that never sleeps ...
P. 8/9 Midtown Manhattan with the Chrysler and Empire State Buildings

DOWNTOWN MANHATTAN · 14

Statue of Liberty · 16
Ellis Island · 18
Staten Island Ferry · 20
Battery Park, Robert F. Wagner Jr Park · 22
Museum of Jewish Heritage –
   a Living Memorial to the Holocaust · 24
Alexander Hamilton U.S. Custom House · 26
South Street Seaport Historic District · 28
Wall Street, New York Stock Exchange (NYSE) · 30
The financial center of the world · 32
Federal Hall National Memorial Building · 34
Trinity Church · 36
World Financial Center (WFC) · 38
"Nine Eleven" · 40
World Trade Center Site (Ground Zero) · 42
St Paul's Chapel · 44
Woolworth Building · 46
Newspaper Row:
   "All the News That's Fit to Print" · 48
Brooklyn Bridge · 50
Civic Center · 56
TriBeCa · 58
Chinatown · 60
Soho · 62
Art and architecture in cast-iron frames · 64
Little Italy · 66
Pizza, pasta and parades:
   the San Gennaro Festival in Little Italy · 68

Lower East Side · 70
Kosher is hip: New York and
   the Jewish avant-garde · 72
Katz's Delicatessen · 74
East Village · 76
Manhattan Bridge · 78
New York's Graffiti · 80
Greenwich Village · 82
Romance in small doses: Sex and the City · 84
Return of the spirits:
   the Village Halloween Parade · 86
Gay Pride: New York over the rainbow · 88
Union Square · 90
Gramercy Park Historic District · 92
Madison Square Park · 94
Flatiron Building · 96
Chelsea · 98
Art and the art of life in New York · 100
Chelsea Hotel · 102
Meatpacking District · 104
Joyce Theater · 106
High Line Park · 108

MIDTOWN · 110

Madison Square Garden · 112
Empire State Building · 114
Skyscrapers and skywalkers · 116
The Morgan Library & Museum · 118
New York Public Library, Bryant Park · 120

Grand Central Terminal	122
Chrysler Building	124
City lights – after hours	126
570 Lexington Avenue	128
United Nations Headquarter	130
Trump World Tower	132
Park Avenue	134
Waldorf-Astoria Hotel	136
St. Patrick's Cathedral	138
Citygroup Center, Lipstick, Sony Tower	140
Broadway	142
Showtime: Live on Broadway	144
Times Square	146
Hot dogs on every corner	152
Avenue of the Americas (Sixth Avenue)	154
New York fashion:	
runways, rags and riches	156
Fifth Avenue	158
Rockefeller Center	160
Top of the Rock	162
Art Déco: decorative art in architecture	164
Radio City Music Hall	166
Soundtrack of the city:	
Sinatra's "New York, New York"	168
All things expensive and beautiful:	
shopping in New York	170
Museum of Modern Art (MoMA)	172
Trump Tower	174
Grand Army Plaza, Plaza Hotel	176

Vanishing point of dreams and aspirations:	
New York's skyline	178
Carnegie Hall	184
Columbus Circle, Time Warner Center	186
CENTRAL PARK	
AND UPPER EAST SIDE	**188**
Bloomingdale's	190
Strawberry Fields forever:	
John Lennon's dream	192
Central Park	194
Metropolitan Museum of Art	200
Frick Collection	202
Whitney Museum of American Art	204
Solomon R. Guggenheim Museum	206
East Harlem	208
East Side Story: Hispanics in New York	210
UPPER WEST SIDE, HARLEM	
AND NORTHERN MANHATTAN	**212**
Lincoln Center for the Performing Arts	214
Metropolitan Opera House	216
Bagel, burger & Zabar's:	
New York culinary delights	218
American Museum of Natural History	220
Columbia University, Cathedral of	
St John the Divine	222

The Cloisters	224
Harlem	226
Abyssinian Baptist Church	228
Harlem shuffle: faith, hope and jazz	230
125th Street	232
Apollo Theatre	234
OUTER BOROUGHS	**236**
DUMBO	238
Brooklyn Heights	240
Coney Island	242
Queens	244
The Bronx	246
Heroes in pinstripes:	
the New York Yankees	248
Bronx Zoo, New York Botanical Garden	250
A long way home:	
the New York City Marathon	252

DOWNTOWN MANHATTAN

New York City is divided into what are referred to as the five boroughs of Manhattan, Brooklyn, Queens, the Bronx, and Staten Island, all of which are home to hundreds of famous neighborhoods like Greenwich Village, SoHo and Harlem. Sandwiched between the Atlantic estuary of the East River and the Hudson, Manhattan Island is simply divided into Downtown (stretching from the southern tip of the island up to 30th Street), Midtown (from 30th Street to Central Park) and Uptown (from Central Park to the far north, into Harlem and Washington Heights).

For New Yorkers, "ups and downs" are not just emotional but geographical as well: going "uptown" in Manhattan means heading north, while "downtown" is heading south. The southern end of the island is home to the buildings that give the city it's recognizable character.

STATUE OF LIBERTY

New York's most iconic monument, the Statue of Liberty, is actually of French origin. It was conceived as a gift to the United States by political activist Edouard René Lefebvre de Laboulaye – an admirer of the American Constitution and a critic of Napoleon III – and sculptor Frédéric-Auguste Bartholdi. The huge statue, which was allegedly inspired by the Colossus of Rhodes and modeled after either the artist's mistress or his mother, was constructed in France and then dismantled and transported to the States in crates. It was finally unveiled at its present site on Liberty Island on 28 October 1886. Now a UNESCO World Heritage Site, the statue's foundations weigh approximately 24,000 tons and her robes conceal a steel frame constructed by Alexandre Gustave Eiffel, who went on to build his famous tower in Paris.

"Give me your tired, your poor / Your huddled masses yearning to breathe free / The wretched refuse of your teeming shore / Send these, the homeless, tempest-tossed to me / I lift my lamp beside the golden door!" This is Miss Liberty's greeting to new arrivals in New York harbor. Her copper sheathing conceals an iron framework designed by Gustave Eiffel.

ELLIS ISLAND

Between 1892 and 1954, roughly 15 million immigrants seeking a new life in America arrived on Ellis Island at the mouth of the Hudson River. Before receiving the sought-after stamp, however, they were all required to pass a multipart test in the now famous red-brick building that was once a munitions depot. The Immigration Museum recalls this period. The last leg of their journey to become an American went from the luggage room up to the second floor where the medical examinations took place. More than 5,000 people waited daily in the Registry Room for the process to be completed. More than 2.5 million of them came from Italy, nearly two million from Russia and roughly 700,000 from Germany. Just two percent of the applications were rejected, and 3,000 people committed suicide here because they did not want to return to their homelands.

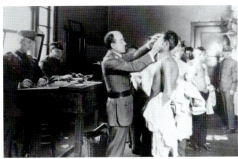

Photographic portraits of hopeful immigrants are arranged into the stylized stripes of an American flag at the Museum of Immigration on Ellis Island (below). The memorabilia housed in the museum also includes antique pieces of luggage. Before being allowed to continue on their journey, prospective immigrants had to undergo tests, questioning and a physical examination (left).

STATEN ISLAND FERRY

The Staten Island Ferry connects the southern tip of Manhattan with Staten Island, which lies out in the bay. About 200 million passengers a year make their way between South Ferry (Whitehall Street) and St George Ferry Terminals. In the 18th century, the short trip was covered by only two private sailboats, but by the 19th century, the first steamships had arrived. A disaster in 1871 killed 85 people when the Westfield's boiler exploded. The ferries have been owned and operated by the City of New York since 1905. In 1897, the 20-minute crossing cost 5 cents, and the price was not changed until 1972, when it became 10 cents. In 1975 it was raised to 25 cents; in 1990 to 50 cents. Since 1997, however, the journey has been free, and there isn't a better way to see downtown Manhattan – the ferry has absolutely magnificent views of the city's skyline and bridges.

This ferry runs round the clock between the southern tip of Manhattan and the northern tip of Staten Island and carries about twenty million commuters and visitors a year. The ride affords fantastic views of the Manhattan skyline and passes by the Statue of Liberty. The ferry boats are painted bright orange in order to make them more visible in foggy weather.

BATTERY PARK, ROBERT F. WAGNER JR PARK

Battery Park lies at the southernmost tip of Manhattan and is the starting point for trips out to the Statue of Liberty and Ellis Island. Its name comes from the Dutch artillery ("batteries") stationed on the coast here during the Colonial period in the 17th century. Next door, Battery Park City and the office blocks of the World Financial Center stand on artificial land reclaimed during the excavation phase for the World Trade Center towers. The Castle Clinton Monument, a fort constructed to defend against the British, is also located in the park. The gap between Battery Park and Battery Park City was filled in during the 1990s with the opening of Robert F. Wagner Jr Park, named after a former mayor of the city. Pier A stretches out into the bay just to the south of the promenade and features a building from 1886 with a tower at the end of it. It was formerly a dock for fire department vessels.

BATTERY PARK, ROBERT F. WAGNER JR PARK

Battery Park (large photo) merges almost imperceptibly into Robert F. Wagner Jr Park while the impressive skyline of Battery Park City rises above (left). Robert F. Wagner Jr (1910–1991) was the son of German immigrants who became mayor of New York from 1954 until 1965. A statue in Battery Park commemorates the explorer Giovanni da Verrazano, who in 1524 was the first European to enter New York harbor.

MUSEUM OF JEWISH HERITAGE – A LIVING MEMORIAL TO THE HOLOCAUST

This museum complex serves as a memorial to the Holocaust and was created by architects Kevin Roche and John Dinkeloo. It opened at the southern end of Battery Park City in 1997 and six years later expanded to include the Robert Morgenthau Wing as well as Andy Goldsworthy's *Garden of Stones*. Its unusual design manages to catch the eye from a distance: a three-storey hexagonal building topped by a six-stepped pyramidal roof.

The number six is a reference to the six-pointed Star of David as well as to the six million Jews who were killed in the Holocaust. Three times six also yields the number eighteen, which stands for the Hebrew word chaim ("life"). This is in keeping with the underlying concept of the museum, which not only commemorates the fate of Jews in the twentieth century, but also aims to give hope for the future.

MUSEUM OF JEWISH HERITAGE – A LIVING MEMORIAL TO THE HOLOCAUST

Nearly 25,000 items are on display here including photos, documents, reports from eyewitnesses as an expression of Jewish cultural heritage (below). For his *Garden of Stones*, London environmental artist Andy Goldsworthy collected eighteen stones from various parts of the northeastern United States and placed a miniature oak tree on top of each one – a symbol of life (and survival) under adverse conditions.

ALEXANDER HAMILTON U.S. CUSTOM HOUSE

Income tax was not actually introduced in the United States until 1913. Until then, excise duty collected by the customs authorities filled the important role of providing the government with revenue, and this was administered in New York from the US Custom House, an elegant building with a Beaux Arts façade designed by Cass Gilbert in 1907 (later architect of the renowned Woolworth Building). Since 1994 the building has housed the Gustav Heye Center of the National Museum of the American Indians, which brilliantly illustrates the history of Native American cultures of North, Central and South America. The heart of the exhibits in the museum can mainly be traced back to the private collection of banker George Gustav Heye (1874–1957), who had already opened his first museum dedicated to Native Americans on the edge of Harlem in 1916.

Since the George Gustav Heye Center of the National Museum of the American Indians moved its collections to the Smithsonian Institution's museum for Native Americans at the end of 2004, its New York premises have been used mainly for temporary exhibits. The building itself is of great architectural interest. The former U.S. Customs House is a granite pile designed by Cass Gilbert with sculptures by Daniel Chester French.

SOUTH STREET SEAPORT HISTORIC DISTRICT

The old port area between Water Street and the East River is now a listed heritage monument. It started in the mid-1960s when a group of citizens calling themselves the "South Street Museum" began collecting boats and buying up dilapidated buildings in the port area. About ten years later, the notion of transforming the area into a living district gained traction, with restored and new buildings, museums, stores and old sailboats, some of which could themselves be museums. Schermerhorn Row, with its warehouses and offices from 1813, is the pride of the port. The Fulton Fish Market has become a shopping mall and a small lighthouse commemorating the sinking of the Titanic in 1912. Pier 17 has three floors of restaurants and stores and a fantastic view of Brooklyn Bridge. The visitors' center has information on activities in the area. It's a great place to come for shopping and dining.

The East River links Long Island Sound with New York Harbor whose water, thanks to the flow of the tides, moves so quickly that in winter it's almost always free of ice. This explains the historic importance of the port as an anchorage for wooden ships (left, the historic four-master Peking). The name of the Fulton Market Building (below) evokes the old fish market here that was moved to the Bronx in 2005.

WALL STREET, NEW YORK STOCK EXCHANGE (NYSE)

The heart of New York's Financial District is Wall Street, which runs along the site of a former wooden defensive wall erected by the Dutch in 1653. Alexander Hamilton, the country's first Secretary of the Treasury, was keen on the idea of making New York a center for stock trading and issued federal government bonds to offset the debts incurred during the War of Independence. Although Wall Street subsequently became synony-mous with finance, it's worth noting that the Stock Exchange is actually located round the corner, on Broad Street, between Wall Street and Exchange Place. In 1936 a marble relief entitled Integrity Protecting the Works of Man was placed above the Corinthian pillars of the façade, representing the Stock Exchange as the index of the nation's wealth; this was later replaced with a lead-covered replica. It's a fascinating area to explore and worth a visit.

The New York Stock Exchange building was designed by George B. Post and built in 1903. It features a façade that very much resembles a classical Greek temple, with a statue of George Washington presiding over it (below). Until 2005, traders on the floor of the stock exchange still shouted out their orders but an electronic trading system was finally installed (left, the 3-D trading floor).

THE FINANCIAL CENTER OF THE WORLD

On 17 May 1792, twenty-four businessmen and bankers met under a plane tree on Wall Street and signed an agreement to regulate the purchase and sale of shares and bonds, thus laying the foundations for the New York Stock Exchange. The "New York Stock & Exchange Board" subsequently extended and formalized these revolutionary rules in 1817, and the current title of the "New York Stock Exchange" was finally adopted in 1863.

Initially, two sessions were held in which the president of the exchange would call out the stocks and members submitted their offers. Each member had their own chair, or "seat" at the exchange, and in 1817 this privilege cost $25. The NYSE is currently the largest stock exchange in the world. It has been state-regulated since 1934 and is run by a private corporation of stock brokers and traders. The oldest stock index is

the Dow Jones Index. Listed on the stock market since 2006 as the NYSE Group, the concern then created "NYSE Euronext, Inc.", the world's first transatlantic stock exchange, in a merger in April 2007. The acquisition of the American Stock Exchange (AMEX) in October 2008 gave rise to the "NYSE Alternext US".

THE FINANCIAL CENTER OF THE WORLD

The heart of the financial world is housed behind a neoclassical façade (far left) and is increasingly being shifted from the trading floor to cyberspace. The free convertibility of the U.S. dollar, i.e. the right to unlimited currency exchange as guaranteed by the Federal Reserve Board, facilitates world trade. Arturo DiModica's *Charging Bull* (left), stands nearby on Bowling Green and inspires optimism on the market.

FEDERAL HALL NATIONAL MEMORIAL BUILDING

Nothing is left of the old New York City Hall, which was first built in 1701 and later remodeled by Pierre L'Enfant. It was on this balcony that George Washington was sworn into office on April 30th, 1789, and where Congress was located during the 1789–1790 session. The building was torn down less than twenty-five years after Washington's oath of office, apparently having been sold a mere 425 dollars. Nothing was built on the site of the "birth-place of the American government" until 1834, when Ithiel Town and Alexander Jackson Davis designed a new building that served first as a customs house, then as a treasury, and finally as a national memorial housing a museum. The building's classical façade is seen as a successful example of Greek Revival, a style influenced by Greek designs, while the central interior rotunda is clearly inspired by Roman models.

Barack Obama (left), the 44th president of the United States, has stated that his role model is Abraham Lincoln, the opponent of oppression and slavery on whose bible he took his oath of office. However, he also owes a debt to the legacy of the first president and founding father of the United States, George Washington, whose statue, designed by J.Q.A. Ward in 1882, stands in front of the memorial (far left).

TRINITY CHURCH

The current Trinity Church, built in 1846 in a neo-Gothic design by Richard Upjohn, was preceded by a series of Anglican churches. The first was built as early as 1698, but burnt down eight years later, in 1706. A second church constructed on the site was consecrated in 1790 but demolished in 1839 for safety reasons. The modern church's bronze doors are reminiscent of Lorenzo Ghiberti's *Gates of Paradise* in the Baptistry in Florence. A bronze by Steve Tobin was placed in front of the church in 2005 to commemorate the tragic events of 9/11. Parts of the church's historic cemetery date back to the 18th century, and it includes the graves of Alexander Hamilton, the first US Secretary of the Treasury, and Robert Fulton, the inventor of the steamship. The church has a museum that hosts special exhibitions throughout the year illustrating the history of the church and the parish.

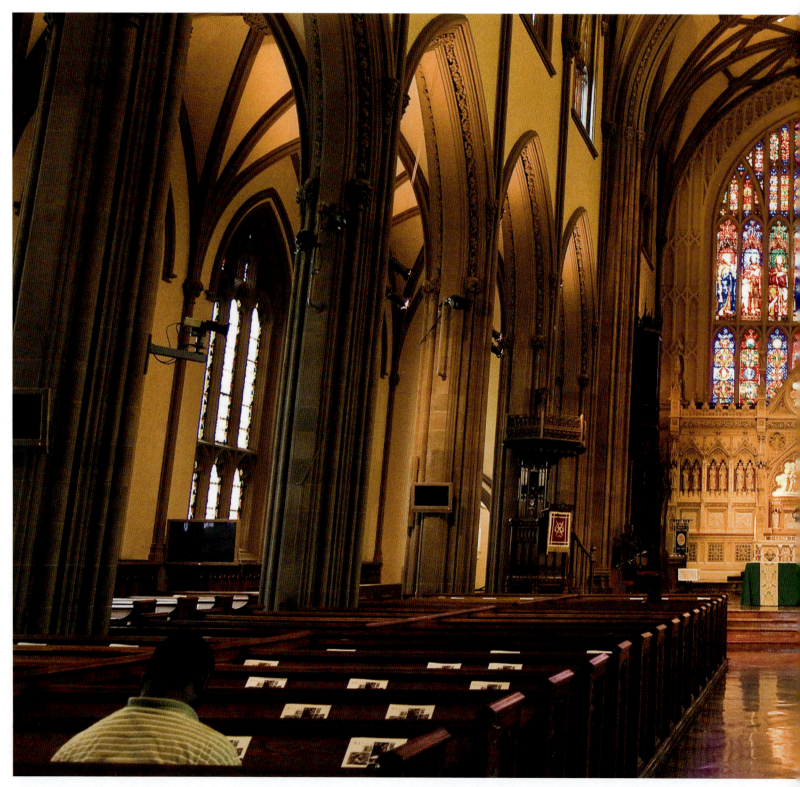

Trinity Church (left) is a triple-aisled sandstone basilica that stands huddled among towering skyscrapers. It features lovely stained glass (below). In 1705, Queen Anne granted the parish possession of the entire area west of Broadway, from Fulton Street northwards up to Christopher Street. The rents received from buildings put up on the property formed the basis for the enormous wealth of the congregation.

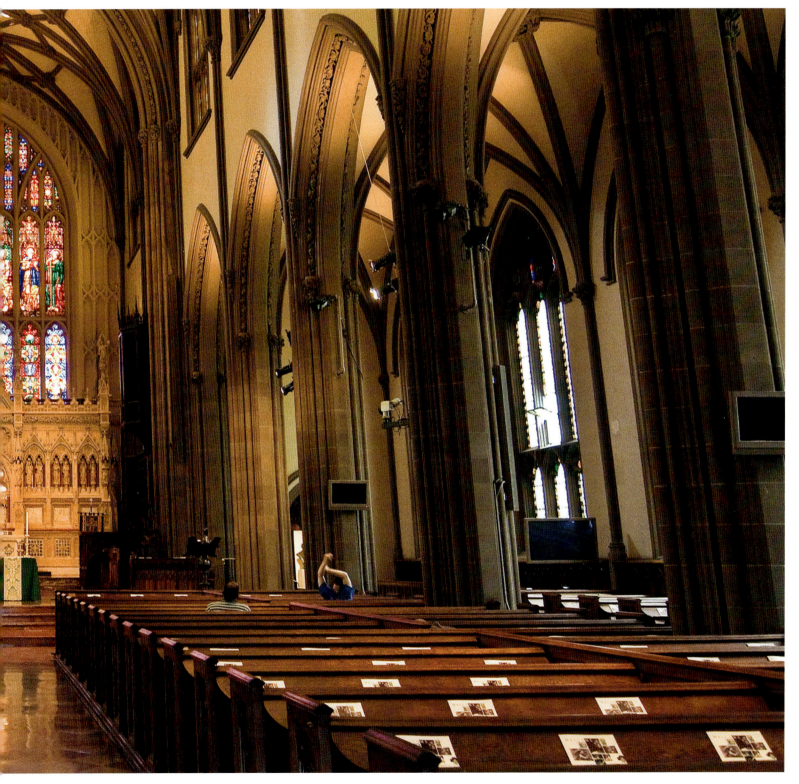

WORLD FINANCIAL CENTER (WFC)

Excavations for the World Trade Center produced enough landfill to create a strip of shoreline on which Battery Park City was built. The hub of the complex, built in the late 1980s based on designs by César Palli, is the World Financial Center. It features four granite and glass office blocks of differing heights with up to fifty-one floors and post-modern copper roofs. Each building reflects a basic architectural form: a truncated pyramid, a cupola, a pyramid, and a ziggurat (stepped pyramid). The façades of towers two and three were badly damaged during the attack on the World Trade Center in 2001, but they were quickly repaired. The WFC has an area of 27,000 sq. m (291,000 sq. feet) and is home to such giants as Dow Jones and American Express. The open plaza has a view of the Hudson River and North Cove Yacht Harbor. Anyone interested in architecture would enjoy a visit, and the view is spectacular.

An enormous gap between the towers of the World Financial Center (left, with its marina on the Hudson river) marks the area where the twin towers of the World Trade Center once soared. The Center, which at its dedication in 1988 was hailed as the "Rockefeller Center of the 21st century", houses shops and restaurants inside its winter garden, with sixteen royal palms from the Mohave Desert adding an exotic touch.

"NINE ELEVEN"

Much of the world held its collective breath on September 11th, 2001, as part of a secretly planned attack on the economic and political centers of the United States was carried out by alleged members of the terrorist organization Al Qaeda. They flew two loaded passenger jets into the twin towers of the World Trade Center: American Airlines flight 11 crashed into the north tower of the World Trade Center at 8:46 a.m., and at 9:03 a.m. a second jet, United Airlines flight 175, flew into the south tower. Fully loaded with fuel, the planes became incendiary bombs and set several floors on fire. Over two thousand people were trapped. Any initial ideas that the first crash was an accident disappeared with the second crash and the news of similar explosions at the Pentagon and in Pennsylvania. Obviously coordinated attacks, the FAA (Federal Aviation Administration) immediately ordered all aircraft to be grounded and a state of emergency was declared in New York. An army of policemen and firefighters was deployed in an attempt to save lives, but their efforts were mostly in vain. At 9:59 a.m. the south tower collapsed, burying under a mountain of rubble not only the people trapped inside, but also many firefighters. The north tower followed at 10.28 a.m. Over 2,700 people died in New York alone.

"I've been in the service for twenty years. I've seen a lot, but what was really bad down there was that you couldn't see anything. No victims, no computers, no telephones, no doors, not even door handles. Do you know how many door handles there were in the World Trade Center? This nothingness – that was terrible." (Lieutenant Peter Glowacz of Engine Company 9 in Chinatown)

WORLD TRADE CENTER SITE (GROUND ZERO)

Built on square foundations to heights of 415 m (1,361 ft) and 417 m (1,368 ft) respectively, the stainless steel Twin Towers of the World Trade Center were the tallest buildings in the world for a few weeks after their completion in 1974. They ceded this title shortly thereafter to the 443-m (1,453-ft) Sears Tower in Chicago. The Twin Towers, each boasting 110 floors, were part of a complex of seven office buildings that were connected to the World Financial Center by an underground passage as well as a bridge. Known as "Ground Zero" since the attack of September 11, 2001, the 6.5-ha (16-acre) site was not even completely cleared of rubble from the destroyed buildings until the summer of 2002. It was originally planned that five new skyscrapers were to be constructed here, but the financial crisis of 2009 resulted in significant revisions to these plans.

Every year on September 11th, two columns of light (the "Tribute to Light") commemorate the terrorist attack (far left). The National September 11 Memorial & Museum Memorial Park was inaugurated on September 11, 2011, the tenth anniversary of the 9/11 attacks (left). A computer rendering shows how One World Trade Center, or simply 1WTC, is set to dominate the cityscape (below).

ST PAUL'S CHAPEL

St Paul's Chapel, once a place of worship for George Washington, was completed in 1776 and is New York's oldest church. It was created by master craftsman Andrew Gautier, who probably based his design on James Gibbs' church of St Martin's in the Fields in London. Apart from the addition of a spire in 1796, the building has remained unchanged since its consecration. When the rubble from the attacks of September 11, 2001, was being cleared, this Episcopal chapel (which belongs to the Anglican church) was used by workers taking breaks. Miraculously, the church was not destroyed during the attack: a nearby tree dissipated the effects of the shockwaves so completely that not even a window pane was broken. Only a stump and the roots of the tree survived, inspiring the sculpture which now stands in front of Trinity Church – Trinity Root by Steve Tobin.

On September 11th, 2001, the World Trade Center, rose in flames directly behind the old cemetery on the west side of St Paul's chapel. Reverend Stuart H. Hoke (left) was one of the survivors of the attack that transformed this house of worship into a memorial. The church was constructed from Manhattan schist and brownstone – New World materials used for an Old World design.

WOOLWORTH BUILDING

On its unveiling in April 1913, the Woolworth Building was hailed as the "Eighth Wonder of the World". Indeed, at 241 m (790 ft) in height it was the world's tallest building (until 1930) and the man who commissioned it, Franklin Winfield Woolworth, never omitted to mention that he had paid for it – all $13.5 million of it – in cash. His rise to department store king had begun with a "five cent store" in Utica, New York. When this went bust he tried his luck in Lancaster, Pennsylvania, extending his range to include goods that also cost ten cents. He opened his first store in New York in 1896 and by the time of his death in 1916 he owned an empire of more than a thousand keenly priced stores around the world – and a personal fortune of $65 million. A relief of him – counting his money – can be found in the lobby of the Woolworth Building, the so-called "Cathedral of Commerce".

The Woolworth Building has been called a "Cathedral of Commerce", but according to its architect, Cass Gilbert, its design was inspired not by religious architecture but by Gothic town halls. The building is not a work of masonry, but instead a steel-frame construction with its lower floors serving as a granite foundation. On the floors above, the steel skeleton is covered by an outer wall of terracotta tiles.

NEWSPAPER ROW: "ALL THE NEWS THAT'S FIT TO PRINT"

Running east from City Hall Park, Park Row was known as "Newspaper Row" in the 19th century. Among the fifteen papers that settled in the Financial District due to its proximity to City Hall was the New York Evening Post, founded by Alexander Hamilton in 1801 (although since 1906 it has been situated in Vesey Street and since 1934 it has appeared under the title "New York Post"). Even the New York Times – whose 1889 motto "All The News That's Fit To Print" still appears on every masthead – was originally based here. Now listed as a national monument, the original New York Times Building (41 Park Row) was designed by George B. Post in 1889. It is currently part of the campus of Pace University, which not so coincidentally offers courses in publishing and computer studies. The headquarters of the various media companies based in New York have long since been scattered across the city, however, leaving Newspaper Row's publishing past commemorated by just one public space: Printing House Square, between Park Row, Nassau and Spruce Streets. It features a statue designed in 1872 by Ernst Plassmann of American founding father Benjamin Franklin clutching a copy of the Pennsylvania Gazette – of which he was the editor.

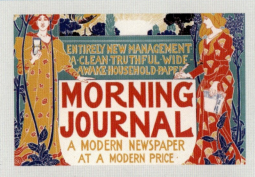

Over 200 newspapers are published in the city, and although electronic competition has made the market more competitive, Arthur Ochs Sulzberger of the New York Times says, "We have to be clear about one thing – as a newspaper, we're not in the paper business, we're in the news business. As long as we define ourselves by the word news, we have a brilliant future ahead of us".

This legendary bridge spanning the East River between Manhattan and Brooklyn was opened in May 1883 after some sixteen years of construction. Not including the approach roads, it is 1,052 m (3,451 ft) in length; including those roads it is 1,825 m (5,987 ft). On its first day of service 150,000 people crossed the bridge. Barnum's Circus even sent a herd of elephants over the bridge to convince sceptics of the structure's stability.

The Brooklyn Bridge was originally designed by German architect John Augustus Roebling, but he died shortly after construction began. His son Washington then took over the challenge with his wife Emily and supervised completion of the first suspension bridge to incorporate steel cables – the monumental construction ultimately required 24,000 km (15,000 mi) of it. It's a truly spectacular feat of engineering.

When it opened, the Brooklyn Bridge was considered a miracle of engineering skill. It was, after all, the world's longest suspension bridge. Pedestrians were invited to enjoy the "Elevated Pleasure Walk", a boardwalk running above the traffic lanes and arguably the most beautiful promenade in the city. An especially lovely view of the Brooklyn Bridge and the Manhattan skyline can be seen from the Clock Tower Building in Brooklyn.

CIVIC CENTER

New York's legal and administrative district – the Civic Center – is south of Chinatown and bound to the west by Broadway and to the east by the East River. Its many public buildings include the famous City Hall, the oldest in the United States and still the city's administrative headquarters. It was constructed between 1803 and 1812 by Joseph François Mangin and John McComb Jr in the "Federal Style" that developed from the "British Colonial Style" after the War of Independence. Throughout the 19th century, the City Hall Park alongside the building had been an open area used for grazing cattle, assemblies and military exercises. The grand Municipal Building is an office block completed in 1914 to accommodate increased space for city administrators and provides an architectural contrast to City Hall. A visit to City Hall as part of a sightseeing tour is highly recommended.

The Civic Center is dominated by the imposing Municipal Building (below). Its dome is an architectural reference to the much smaller City Hall (left), which is crowned by a gilded statue called *Civic Fame* representing the unification of the five boroughs into one city. Opposite City Hall stands the memorial to Nathan Hale, who in 1776 was hanged by the British for being "the first American spy".

TRIBECA

TriBeCa (the "Triangle Below Canal Street") is another example of how New York continually reinvents itself. In the mid-1970s this was a run-down industrial area known as the "Lower West Side", until a property developer recognized the potential of its many empty factories and warehouses and came up with the catchy new moniker. His gamble paid off: TriBeCa was suddenly "cool" and many artists from nearby SoHo relocated their ateliers, studios, and rehearsal rooms because the rents were comparatively cheap. TriBeCa has remained trendy but is now also expensive, and the in-crowd has long since moved on. The triangle of streets between West Broadway, Canal West, and Chambers streets now encloses more restaurants than galleries – including some of the best in the city – and they make a great place for relaxing and recuperating after a day spent exploring.

Hollywood star Robert De Niro has invested much of his time and money into TriBeCa (below left, a typical row of buildings). He was the driving force behind the annual TriBeCa Film Festival, and is co-owner of the Tribeca Grill (below). Along with partner Nobu Matsuhisa (left, at the one-Michelin-star Nobu New York restaurant), he has also brought Japanese haute cuisine to TriBeCa.

CHINATOWN

The Chinese enclave south of Canal Street is now home to about 200,000 predominantly Chinese people, the largest Asian community outside Asia. All the signs are written in Chinese characters and the smell of Peking duck and exotic sauces wafts from the open doorways. Thanks to its 200-plus restaurants, more than 300 flourishing textile and clothing firms, numerous shops and grocery stores, and seven daily Chinese newspapers, Chinatown is an independent city within Manhattan. The Buddhist Temple of America is located on Mott Street and the Church of the Transfiguration, built in 1801 and Catholic since 1850 (once an important focus for Irish and Italian immigrants) has had a Chinese priest since 1970. The infamous "Bloody Angle", the scene of violent skirmishes between rival Chinese street gangs (known as the "Tong Wars"), is over on Doyers Street.

Manhattan's Chinatown emerged during the 1870s in the area bordered by Canal, Baxter, Worth and Park streets, and in the Bowery, but it has long since outgrown this and is today a "city within the city". To the north it already takes up a large part of Little Italy, pushing almost as far as SoHo. Where the Jewish community of the Lower East Side once lived you can now sometimes hear more Chinese spoken than English.

SOHO

According to former mayor Ed Koch, an artist's role in New York is "to make a district so attractive that the artists can't afford to live there any more." And it's the real estate broker's job, one might add, to package it attractively. Like TriBeCa, the abbreviation SoHo ("South of Houston") has commercial roots referring to an industrial area south of Houston Street once known as the "South Village". In the 1960s, the area, which had largely been aban- doned and dilapidated, began to attract artists and bohemian types who quickly moved into the empty loft spaces and deserted factory buildings – at least until Ed Koch's prediction was truly fulfilled. Soho has now become a trendy area famous for its destination shopping. It's a great place for exploring antique stores and unusual galleries and for admiring a wonderful, unique collection of cast-iron architecture.

An up-and-coming neighborhood with art galleries and original antique shops awaits visitors to SoHo. The most interesting shops can be found in Prince Street (far left, Prada), on West Broadway (left, Stefano Gabbana and Domenico Dolce in their shop) and in Spring Street. Water tanks (below) are a necessity when the pressure in New York water pipes doesn't reach the top floors.

ART AND ARCHITECTURE IN CAST-IRON FRAMES

SoHo's charming streets also have a long tradition of combining art and architecture. However, it is one that was long neglected until a revival in the 1960s, and would have dwindled to nothing had conservationists not realized the rarity value of the cast-iron houses that are common to the neighborhood. Fortunately, many have now even been restored. Cast iron became a popular building material in the 19th century because it was much lighter and cheaper to work than stone or brick, and it permitted the architect to prefabricate decorative features and façades in the foundry and then have them bolted together on site like plates. Cast iron was also prized for its resistance to fire. The era of cast-iron buildings only really ended with the construction of steel-framed skyscrapers in the 1890s, and New York retains the world's greatest concentration of façades wholly or partly constructed of cast iron. The most beautiful houses are, unsurprisingly, in the Cast Iron District between West Broadway, West Houston Street, Canal Street and Crosby Street. Green Street, at the heart of the district, has more than fifty such buildings spread across five blocks, all built between 1869 and 1895. This is certainly the area to come for students of architecture.

Appearances can be deceiving: in SoHo, what often looks like marble, tile or sandstone is actually cast iron. The load-bearing outer walls of these buildings were constructed as cast-iron frameworks made up of individual interlocking elements (beams and struts). They don't, however, provide protection against fires, which is why the buildings all had to be equipped with fire escapes (left and below).

LITTLE ITALY

"I grew up in a world that was much more European than American," said director Martin Scorsese, who grew up in Little Italy like his acting alter ego, Robert de Niro. Scorsese was raised in part by his grandparents, illiterate Sicilian farmers who spoke no English and who, like many southern Italians in the 19th century, had left conditions of poverty to emigrate to New York. They joined some 40,000 other Italians living in a district stretching from Canal Street to Houston Street. It was a world of its own that now exists only in films. Modern-day Little Italy is among Manhattan's smallest ethnic quarters, with just 5,000 Italians living in about four blocks; the rest have moved on, to Brooklyn or the Bronx. If you visit the area in the middle of September during the local festival, you may think you have been transported to Italy itself. This is the area to come for authentic Italian food.

The legend lives on – even if "Little Italy" is constantly being encroached on by a mercilessly expanding Chinatown. Nowadays, the original atmosphere of this Italian enclave continues mostly in its restaurants and small shops. Two of the most traditional Italian restaurants are Puglia in Hester Street (below left), and Lombardi's (left), the oldest pizzeria in the United States from 1905.

PIZZA, PASTA AND PARADES: THE SAN GENNARO FESTIVAL IN LITTLE ITALY

A majority of the estimated four million Italians who emigrated to the United States between 1820 and 1920 came from poor regions in southern Italy. So it comes as no surprise during the ten-day street fair in Little Italy in September that the patron saint carried in a grand procession amid pizza, sausages and street vendors comes from southern Italy. To be more exact, the patron saint is from Naples. The relevant entry in the Catholic Encyclopedia gives the name Saint Januarius, in Italian San Gennaro, and according to tradition he was a bishop of Naples who was beheaded in the year 305 during the persecution of the Christians under the reign of Diocletian. He had survived previous ordeals of martyrdom including being put into a burning furnace and coming out unscathed, and being thrown to wild animals who, instead of tearing him to pieces, lay at his feet like gentle lambs. However, the saint is mainly famous for his connection to the "miracle of the blood", which has been repeated for centuries. Along with other relics of the saint, the cathedral of San Gennaro in Naples keeps glass ampoules said to contain the dried blood of the martyr. On the feast days of Januarius, the blood usually liquefies – should the miracle not occur, this is taken as an omen of coming misfortune.

PIZZA, PASTA AND PARADES: THE SAN GENNARO FESTIVAL IN LITTLE ITALY

During the "Feast of San Gennaro" the aroma of sausages and pizza wafts through the streets of Little Italy. Mulberry Street, where Italian immigrants first celebrated their patron saint, is renamed "Via San Gennaro". Since its beginnings on September 19th, 1926, the feast has evolved into a nearly two-week long spectacle where Italians pay homage to a dead man and celebrate their own lives.

LOWER EAST SIDE

At the beginning of the 20th century, Manhattan's Lower East Side – the district between the Bowery and Clinton, East Houston and Canal streets – had the largest Jewish community in the world. These immigrants lived in generally appalling conditions in six- or seven-floor tenements. They were often squashed into tiny, windowless rooms and shared dilapidated cupboards and rusty washbasins with one single toilet in the hallway. It was so hot in summer that many residents slept on the roof. The Tenement Museum in Orchard Street commemorates the difficult conditions experienced by immigrants in the neighborhood. The district still has some 300 synagogues and a few Jewish stores, but most of New York's Jewish population now lives outside Manhattan. This multicultural area now boasts a fascinating range of fashion and food stores as well as interesting market stalls.

"Everybody ought to have a Lower East Side in their life," opined songwriter Irving Berlin, who grew up – apparently happily – in the neighborhood that today is inhabited mainly by Hispanics and Asians. Tenement houses rising several stories high still dominate the area. In the Lower East Side Museum (left) visitors are plunged into the atmosphere of crowded living conditions circa 1900.

KOSHER IS HIP: NEW YORK AND THE JEWISH AVANT-GARDE

New York has the largest Jewish community in the world with about one million living here – more than in Jerusalem. The first twenty-three refugees of Sephardic origin – who were descendants of Jews expelled from Spain in 1492 – reached the New World in 1654, landing their ship at what was to become Battery Park, where there is still a memorial to "The Jewish Plymouth Rock". German, Eastern European, Russian and Ukrainian Jews then followed in several waves of immigration throughout the 19th and 20th centuries. Their descendants have long since become an intrinsic part of American society, allowing the young Jewish avant-garde the freedom to move on from inherited stereotypes and traditions. Founded in 2002, the magazine "Heeb" (once an anti-Semitic term of abuse, from "Hebe", an abbreviation of "Hebrew") has become the organ of this new consciousness, expressing its sense of irony with t-shirts reading "Jews Kick Ass". Film director Steven Spielberg was one of its early backers. Its approach is no-holds-barred satire. Artists like hiphopper Aviad Cohen and filmmaker Jonathan Kesselman, whose *Hebrew Hammer* depicts the first Jewish action hero fighting evil (in this case, Father Christmas' son), are some of the new protagonists of Jewish pop culture.

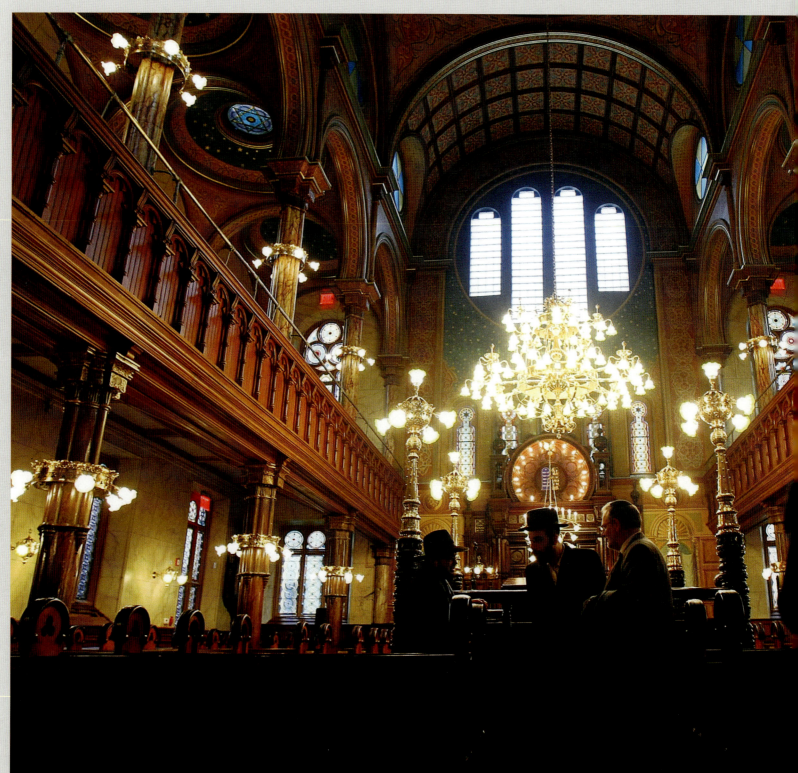

The Jewish influence on city life is unmistakable (below, the Eldridge Street Synagogue, restored in 2007). Everyday Jewish life includes not only the Ultra-Orthodox (far left), who maintain the traditions of the Shtetl (including the distinctive clothing), but also the largely secularized Jews who are recognizable only when they wear yarmulkes on High Holy Days.

KATZ'S DELICATESSEN

Delicatessens are a New York institution, and although the original German word actually refers to "fine foods", modern delis are more akin to fast-food joints selling takeaway as well as offering a variety of dishes to eat between main meals – an overstuffed pastrami sandwich, for example. The most famous of these establishments is probably Katz' Delicatessen, which was opened by an immigrant family on the Lower East Side (205 Houston Street) way back in 1888. The restaurant has since achieved not only culinary, but also cinematic fame: It is here in *When Harry Met Sally* that Meg Ryan provides Billy Crystal with irrefutable proof that a woman can convincingly fake an orgasm – even if it has to be during a date in a deli. The look she then gives him from across the table is unforgettable.

Today, you can still see the table in Katz's Deli where Meg Ryan's "Sally" taught Billy Crystal's "Harry" a very convincing lesson in feminine acting abilities. The deli serves up burgers and grilled meats along with soups, salads and, some say, the best sandwiches in town. The establishment is particularly proud of "Katz's salami" which, like all the other specialties of the house, you can have delivered to your home.

EAST VILLAGE

The northern section of the Lower East Side was already known as the "East Village" by the 1950s, and nowadays the whole area east of Broadway between 14th and Houston Street bears the name. The area where Peter Stuyvesant once owned land was first inhabited by elite families – the Astors and the Vanderbilts of 19th-century New York high society. Immigrants of differing nationalities later moved into the area, which became a place for beatniks and would-be beatniks in the middle of the 20th century. Allen Ginsberg, Jack Kerouac and other such literary giants gave readings wherever a podium could be found, and John Coltrane played his heart out in smoky jazz clubs. The hippies followed, succeeded by the punks, and even today the East Village, where artists like Keith Haring and Jeff Koons first came to prominence is a home for an authentic avant-garde.

"Alphabet City", one of the hippest neighbor-hoods in town, is in the eastern part of the East Village and gets its name from avenues A, B, C and D that run through it. Take a walk around the area (left, the corner of 3rd Ave. and 13th St.; below, three street views) and you'll discover everything from discount CDs to souvenirs. It is also the right place if you want to get your hair done or add a tattoo to your collection.

MANHATTAN BRIDGE

New York is a city of bridges: According to the official count, there are 2,027, seventy-six crossing bodies of water and eighteen connecting Manhattan with the outer boroughs or New Jersey. The first bridge, King's Bridge, was built in 1693 and connected Manhattan with Spuyten Duyvil in present-day Bronx. The oldest existing bridge is High Bridge, built between 1837 and 1848. It extends in thirteen arches over the Harlem River and connects West 174th/175th Streets with the Bronx. Of the three suspension bridges linking downtown Manhattan with Brooklyn, the most recently built is the Manhattan Bridge which, after the Brooklyn Bridge (1883) and the Williamsburg Bridge (1902), opened to traffic on December 13, 1909. Pedestrians have once again been able to cross it since 2001, when renovation work was finished, and a new bicycle lane was opened on the bridge in 2004.

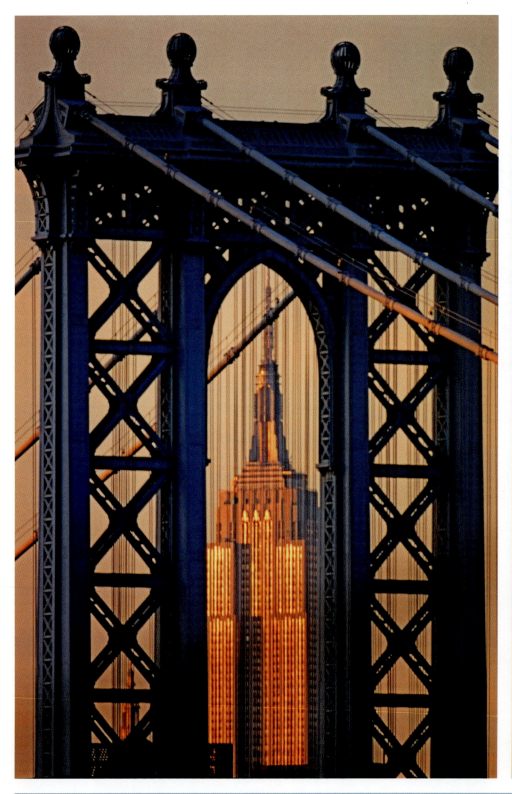

This bridge has a total length of 2,089 m (6,853 ft) with its greatest continuous span reaching 448 m (1,470 ft). It starts at Manhattan's Confucius Plaza and ends in DUMBO in Brooklyn. It was originally designed to carry rail traffic, but nowadays carries car traffic and an elevated line of the subway. It was designed by Leon Solomon Moiseiff working for the architectural firm Carrere & Hastings.

NEW YORK'S GRAFFITI

New York is rightfully considered the cradle of contemporary graffiti, which also helps explain why the city has traditionally fought against it with such vigor. "The more difficult it gets to spray something, the more famous the artist becomes". Following this rule of thumb, New York, especially in 1970s and 1980s, turned into an El Dorado for sprayers, who would at the very least leave their "tags" (the sprayer's pseudonym) on walls or, in the best of situations, cover an entire subway car. Was this art or vandalism? For New York's mayors the answer was clearly the latter and from the beginning they used draconian measures to combat the trend. John Lindsay introduced the first anti-graffiti laws as far back as 1972, and in 1985 Ed Koch prohibited the sale of spray cans. In the 1990s Rudolph Giuliani declared the "production of graffiti" to be a punishable offense. Following the maxim, "the more danger, the more honor", the sprayers saw each new step as a challenge to overcome, a concept that the city authorities haven't seemed to grasp up to now. As recently as 2006, one of the veterans of the graffiti scene, Alan "Ket" Maridueña, was brought before the courts for having defaced several subway cars, twenty years after the now established artist and graphic designer had worked the subways.

Art dealers still chisel artwork off walls that were once considered damaged property in order to sell the works at hefty price tags to wealthy collectors such as Brad Pitt. Some stars of the movement – Keith Haring, Jean-Michel Basquiat, and Richard Hambleton – have been granted museum exhibits, which has encouraged "urban art twins" Os Gemeos to develop their own style between graffiti and muralismo (large photo).

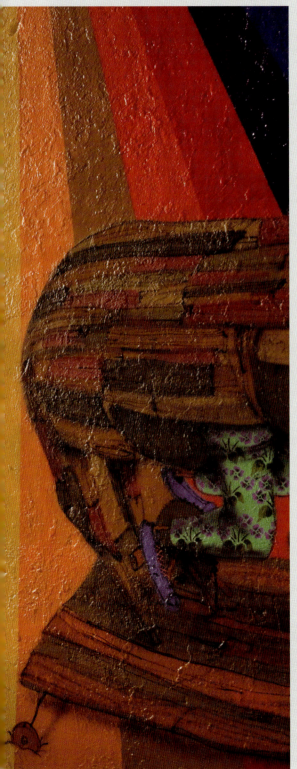

GREENWICH VILLAGE

Greenwich Village is what New Yorkers call the area between 14th Street, Houston Street, the Hudson River and Broadway – "the Village" for short. Indeed, the area's winding, tree-lined streets and alleys still give the impression of the village it was when it was founded in 1696. In 1822 the area expanded when many New Yorkers fleeing a yellow fever epidemic settled further downtown. However, thirteen years later, in 1835, it could still claim to be "an ideal of peaceful and respectable living", if Henry James's description in his novel Washington Square is to be believed. In 1913, journalist John Reed, who later founded the first Communist party in the United States, clambered up the triumphal arch in Washington Square to declare the "Independent Republic of Greenwich Village". No visit is complete without some time spent in this lively and unique corner of New York.

A stroll through Greenwich Village reveals handsome townhouses on idyllic tree-lined streets. Washington Square may not be its geographical center, but it is the pulsating heart of the neighborhood where a large and diverse crowd feels at home. The square, dominated by a triumphal arch commemorating the 100th anniversary of George Washington's inauguration, also attracts many street musicians.

ROMANCE IN SMALL DOSES: SEX AND THE CITY

What could you possibly say about a TV series in which the leading characters are four women and the male characters are relegated to supporting roles? Well, if you're a man, it's better not to say anything at all and to just sit there next to your wife or girlfriend and to be careful not to laugh at the wrong moments. Women who watch the series know exactly when to laugh, because they've always known what it's about. After six seasons, running from 1998 to 2002, a total of ninety-four episodes, and two movies in 2008 and 2010 that were big hits around the world, women are likely more familiar with the show's main characters than they are with the men sitting next to them watching. Sarah Jessica Parker plays Carrie Bradshaw, a journalist whose newspaper column "Sex and the City" gives its name to the series and is itself based on a book by Candace Bushnell. Kim Cattrall is Samantha Jones, a pleasure-seeking PR consultant; Kristin Davis is Charlotte York, an art dealer who can't wait to get married and have children; and Cynthia Nixon is Miranda Hobbes, a lawyer whose attitude is more than a bit cynical. What's the link connecting these four figures? Sex. And then there's a fifth leading character, never directly introduced, but always present: the "City", which is also feminine, of course.

Sarah Jessica Parker (below right, with her actor colleague Cynthia Nixon during the filming of *Sex and the City 2*) doesn't only work a lot in New York; she also lives there, in Brooklyn. By the way, of the four leads in this sex-obsessed series – the storyline rarely gets very romantic – Cynthia Nixon is the only one who was actually born and raised in New York.

RETURN OF THE SPIRITS: THE VILLAGE HALLOWEEN PARADE

Rosy-cheeked women with giant busts, blinking skeletons, scary ghosts, fabulous animals, lavish dragons, garish drag queens, dancing princes, screaming witches and grinning devils – the Village Halloween Parade has become to Manhattan what Carnival is to Rio. Every year on October 31st more than 50,000 masked New Yorkers and an estimated two million visitors celebrate the return of the spirits. According to Celtic legend, they are allowed to pass among the living only on All Hallows' Eve – and they do! The first parade in October 1973 was just a small procession organized by a company making masks in Greenwich Village. The following year, after the Theater for the New City decided to get involved, several thousand masked people were singing and dancing along Sixth Avenue, and since 1975 the Village Halloween Parade has been an event of spectacular proportions. Merry New Yorkers in the oddest costumes follow giant "puppets" crafted from plastic and papier-mâché and dance to cheerful rhythms supplied by a wide variety of bands. Furthermore, even after the terrorist attacks of 9/11, New Yorkers refused to miss out on the parade. Rudolf Giuliani, the mayor at the time, called the parade an "opportunity for healing" for the city, and the theme that year was the phoenix, rising from the ashes.

RETURN OF THE SPIRITS: THE VILLAGE HALLOWEEN PARADE

On the night before All Saints' Day, "All Hallows' Eve" – popularly known in North America as Halloween – even the cops are unusually relaxed about the not exactly G-rated goings on in the Village. Maybe it has to do with ancient Celtic tradition, according to which the souls of those who died in the past year are allowed to return home briefly on this day. Everybody knows the scary, crazy fun will soon be over.

GAY PRIDE: NEW YORK OVER THE RAINBOW

Before June 28, 1969, gays and lesbians were more likely to hide their sexuality than to celebrate it. In most bars and cafés they were in fact less welcome than non-whites. Even Greenwich Village, one of the last enclaves of counterculture, was more tolerant of race than it was of sexuality. Of all people, it was the Mafia that ended up improving things by buying the Stonewall Inn in Christopher Street and turning it into a gay and lesbian bar. Everything was done very discreetly, of course. A bouncer inspected any new arrivals through a peephole, and to buy alcohol you had to become a "club member". Most importantly, no resistance was offered to the regular monthly raids by the police – at least not until June 28, 1969. During this particular raid, a group of gays and lesbians took to the streets and openly resisted the police for the first time. They sang "We Shall Overcome", a popular anthem of the black civil rights movement, and found a new self-image: gay pride. The first gay and lesbian parade to Central Park then took place in the summer of 1970. "Christopher Street Day" is now celebrated around the world. The former Stonewall Inn at 51 Christopher Street, is now a listed heritage monument. The parade is now a huge and exciting event, and visitors come from around the world to take part.

"Undress him, bathe him, and bring him to my tent," was what Cher allegedly said once during her wilder days when some passerby had caught her eye. It's quite possible that the words of the singer-actress-celebrity were in the mind of her double during the planning of a show at "Lips" on Bank Street –"The Ultimate in Drag Dining", according to its ads. Below is "Cindy Lauper" and left is "Whitney Houston".

UNION SQUARE

The name of this square has actually nothing to do with labor unions or the labor movement, even though the square itself has been repeatedly used as a gathering point for political rallies and demonstrations since at least the time of the Civil War (1861 to 1865), and since the first decade of the twentieth century as the site of a "speakers' corner" similar to the one in Hyde Park in London. In fact, the name of the square comes from the "union" of two streets: Broadway and the Bowery. The originally tranquil gardens, which in the 19th century were still private property, have evolved into a well-frequented public refuge from urban living, where office workers have lunch, inline skaters practice stunts, and various types of markets do their daily business. On the site on Union Square West where Andy Warhol's "Factory" opened there is now a large bookstore.

The statue of George Washington in the middle of the park was designed by Henry Kirke Browne and erected in 1856. The Greenmarket is one of the most popular farmers' markets in the city. The streets around Union Square was once home to the first American film studios – an "east coast Hollywood" – during the era of silent movies. The studios later moved west to Los Angeles because of the milder climate.

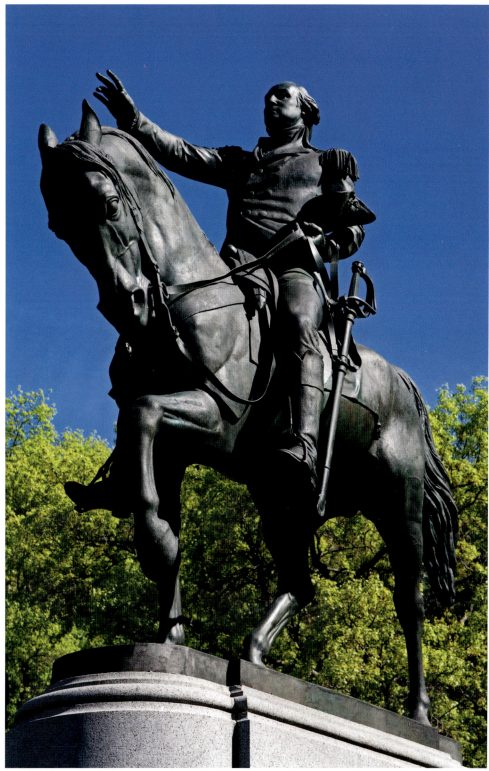

GRAMERCY PARK HISTORIC DISTRICT

At the beginning of the 1830s, a successful investor named Samuel P. Ruggles developed plans for the construction of sixty-six residential buildings arranged around a central green space on land he had acquired. Only future tenants of the development would have access to the park, an idea that was considered a sweetener at the time to attract buyers that has since made Gramercy Park unique. It is the only private park in New York. An address on the park has always been a mark of exclusivity: Samuel J. Tilden, elected governor of New York in 1874, moved into 15 Gramercy Park South (since 1906, home of the National Arts Club); the house next door, number 16, once housed the Players Club, a private club for theater people. In 1966, the neighborhood was declared a Historic District, and in 1988 its boundaries were extended from East 18th to beyond 21st Street.

Today, Gramercy Park (left) is still only accessible to the residents of the buildings around it, with the exception of guests in the Gramercy Park Hotel (below), which opened in 1925 and was where Humphrey Bogart once married. The hotel was designed by Robert T. Lyons and remodeled by Ian Schrager. It is worth having a glance at the lobby, which itself resembles an art gallery.

MADISON SQUARE PARK

Another sanctuary of greenery is Madison Square Park. Named after James Madison, 4th president of the United States, the park is located between Fifth and Madison Avenues from 23rd to 26th Streets. It has existed as a public space since 1686, but wasn't officially declared a public park until 1847. Two years prior, Alexander Cartwright founded the New York Knickerbockers, the first officially documented baseball club and the reason many people consider Madison Square Park to be the birthplace of this quintessential national sport. Until New York's population exploded after the Civil War, the park was considered the northern boundary of the city. Long neglected, the park owes its present appearance as a green oasis to an extensive renovation that was completed in 2001 and cost six million dollars. The funds were collected from public and private sources by the Madison Square Park Conservancy.

The park (left, a statue of Governor William H. Seward) is surrounded by architectural land-marks like the Metropolitan Life Insurance Building, with its Campanile of Venice-inspired tower and which for four years (1909–1913) was the tallest building in the world. In 1876, the arm and torch of the Statue of Liberty were on display in the park where they remained for six years to help raise money to erect the statue.

FLATIRON BUILDING

The Flatiron Building was originally called the Fuller Building and caused a sensation even as it was being completed in 1902. The architects, Daniel Burnham and John Wellborn Root, used the wedge-shaped parcel of land at the intersection of 23rd Street, Fifth Avenue and Broadway to its full extent by erecting a similarly wedge-shaped skyscraper with a steel frame whose design was revolutionary for the time. Clad in light limestone and terracotta, and only 2 m (6.5 ft) wide at its front, the building resembled a giant pressing iron and was known ever after as the "Flatiron Building". Its shape, caused by Broadway's diagonal course through an otherwise grid-based city plan, has meant that this 86-m-high (282-ft) building with twenty-two floors has remained one of the best-known and most photographed skyscrapers in New York as well as one of its iconic landmarks.

The Flatiron Building has attained its iconic status without the help of superlatives. It was never the tallest building in the city, but its distinctive form has always been fascinating. Its type of construction called for a steel skeleton outlining its basic shape, onto which walls and floors of cement were added. This ensured the high degree of stability of the structure.

CHELSEA

In the middle of the 18th century, Chelsea was a farm belonging to a retired English marine officer, Thomas Clark, who had named it after the famous Royal Military Hospital in London. Nowadays this area, bound by 14th and 34th Streets, and Sixth Avenue and the Hudson River, is one of the most attractive and desirable addresses in New York. Chelsea's historic charm, some of which is still visible today, is due in part to writer Clement Clarke Moore. The grandson of Thomas Clarke, he inherited the land and sold it with the idea of creating a mostly not-for-profit, family-friendly building policy. The results were, and indeed still are, unmistakable: the pretty terraces in Chelsea's Historic District have regularly been acclaimed as the nicest in New York and it is simply a very pleasant area for a leisurely stroll. Try guessing which stars live in which houses.

The rows of townhouses in the Chelsea Historic District were built in the mid-19th century. They are often referred to as "brownstones" due to the use of brown sandstone in their construction. The residential character of the area is accentuated by its many small shops. The Empire Diner on Tenth Avenue, allegedly a favorite of Betty Davis, has a sparkling chrome interior which is a jewel of Art Deco styling.

ART AND THE ART OF LIFE IN NEW YORK

New York is a vibrant city, continually changing and always exciting, and there is no better place to witness this than in its art. New York affords its artists more freedom and offers more inspiration than most other cities in the world. However, "art needs patrons", as Viennese composer Otto M. Zykan once said, and that was true long before the latest financial crisis. It is little wonder, perhaps, that it was in New York that pop artists such as Andy Warhol blurred the lines between art and artisan, and former graffiti artists such as Keith Haring turned their hand to both art and merchandizing. Art in New York has to be affordable, and so many artists have had to adapt. This is especially true of female artists like Charline von Heyl, who was Jörg Immendorf's assistant and a member of Martin Kippenberger's circle. Since 1996, she has been part of the New York scene, described by the Village Voice as revolutionary and exceptional in that she is firstly a woman, secondly a painter, thirdly an abstract painter, and fourthly over thirty-five years old. However, while she may have an atypical career, her paintings typically reflect New York in their vibrancy and dynamism. Visit some galleries and seek out the latest developments in New York's endlessly energetic and constantly evolving art scene during your stay.

The best art galleries can be found in Chelsea, which fancies itself the "Gallery Capital of the World". There are many artists working around the galleries, such as the critically acclaimed Charline von Heyl. She was born in Mainz in Germany in 1960, but has been based in New York for the last ten years (below, her studio; right, a photo gallery on West 25th Street).

In her book *Just Kids*, Patti Smith dedicates an entire chapter to the Chelsea Hotel, and it begins with her waiting in the hotel lobby for William Burroughs. She's sitting and observing the comings and goings: "The usual guys with guitar cases and totally spaced out beauties in Victorian clothes. Junkie poets, playwrights, bankrupt filmmakers and French actresses. Everyone who walks through here is a somebody, even when outside they're a nobody." The special "Chelsea" aura attracted Dylan, Hemingway, Hendrix, Lennon and many other famous artists who have called it home; the most tragic celebrity was probably Sid Vicious of the Sex Pistols, who first lost his girlfriend Nancy here before he himself died of a drug overdose in his hotel room months later. The hotel still counts many artists among its long-term residents; only about 100 of its 400 rooms are rented by tourists.

The ten-story brick building on 23rd Street was constructed in 1884 as private apartments. At the time, it was the tallest building in Manhattan. It wasn't transformed into a hotel until the beginning of the twentieth century and it has been listed on the National Register of Historic Places since 1977. According to Patti Smith, the lobby features "bad art" given to the hotel manager in lieu of the rent.

MEATPACKING DISTRICT

The Meatpacking District is on Manhattan's West Side and consists of around twenty blocks between Chelsea Market to the north and Gansevoort Street to the south. Traditionally, it was where butchers worked, hence the district's name. In around 1900, there were as many as 250 abattoirs and warehouses here. In the 1980s, drug dealers and prostitutes moved into the dark alleys and the area's reputation plummeted, a situation that only changed in the 1990s when designers, artists and writers discovered the area. Famous fashion designers such as Diane von Fürstenberg and Christian Louboutin as well as "hip" firms such as Apple, opened branches here. They were followed by restaurants such as Pastis and the Buddha Bar as well as night clubs like Tenjune, One, and Cielo. Put the Meatpacking District on the itinerary for atmosphere and (window) shopping.

Nowadays, there are more designer boutiques than slaughterhouses in the Meat-packing District, whose dark streets would have been avoided by the rich and famous not too many years ago. If you're willing to splurge, get a room in the Hotel Gansevoort and enjoy a view of the neighborhood from the rooftop pool terrace (below). Then have a gander at the special offers like "Naughty but Nice".

JOYCE THEATER

The Joyce Theater on Eighth Avenue in the Meatpacking District is probably one of the best addresses for dance in its most attractive forms, ballet and modern dance. Founded in 1982 "for dancers, by dancers", the Joyce chose as its main venue the Elgin Theater, a movie house built in 1941, which during a two-year remodeling period was entirely gutted in order to create a new 472-seat theater that would meet the technical needs of a modern dance company. Thankfully, the beautiful Art Deco brick façade of the original building was kept. Today, a constant stream of international dance companies visits the theater along with its SoHo branch, which opened in 1996 in a three-story former firehouse and includes two rehearsal studios and an additional 74-seat performance space.

When "Les Ballets Trockadero de Monte Carlo" first performed in the Joyce Theater in 2008, the New York Times wrote that its performance had made "the world into a more beautiful place". Enthusiastic write-ups like this one are probably the dream of dance companies that perform here. Clockwise from far left: Kevin Wynn Collection, Elliot Feld's Mandance Project, Ballet Tech, Tamango's Urban Tap, Parsons Dance.

HIGH LINE PARK

The fact that High Line Park has inspired journalists to lyrical flights of the imagination – it has been called, among other things, a "sun terrace on stilts" or a "green catwalk" – should come as no surprise. Indeed, it should be quite obvious. How does one describe a park that is commonly referred to as being elevated, not simply in the sense of "raised", but in the sense of "exalted"? Everybody agrees on one thing, anyway: the park is New York's newest attraction. Even when you think of how prone New Yorkers are to superlatives, you have to admit the statement is true on two counts: the park, which was created on an unused stretch of elevated rail tracks and opened in 2009 (to be expanded in 2011), is certainly new; and it is most certainly an attraction to walk along the old rails, now planted and green, and enjoy the view. Maybe you'll also feel a bit elevated yourself.

Thanks to the "Friends of the High Line" initiative, a community-based non-profit group, a place where mainly freight trains once traveled (between 1934 and 1980) is now a green ribbon of serenity in the midst of the urban rush. It extends from Gansevoort Street in the Meatpacking District up to 20th Street, but an extension to 30th Street is due to open in 2011 and another reaching 34th Street is being planned.

MIDTOWN

New York's heartbeat is loudest and fastest in central Manhattan, where you can really feel the pulse of time. Gigantic towering skyscrapers like the Empire State, the Chrysler Building and the Trump Tower make deep canyons of the streets. Historic buildings like Grand Central Terminal and the New York Public Library are omnipresent reminders of the city's eventful history. Fifth Avenue revels in luxury, a mecca for chic shoppers and footsore tourists alike, and the bright neon lights of Times Square and Broadway sparkle with life even during the day in the "city that never sleeps".

The spires of the Chrysler and Empire State Buildings stand out amidst the grandiose backdrop of skyscrapers. The sight of it is surpassed only by the sensation of finally plunging into midtown Manhattan, the noisy, pulsating heart of the city.

MADISON SQUARE GARDEN

"The World's Most Famous Arena" is how Madison Square Garden now advertises itself. This multifunction venue, built on Pennsylvania Plaza in 1968, is home to the New York Rangers ice hockey team and the New York Knicks basketball squad. Even the world-famous "Ringling Brothers and Barnum and Bailey Circus" has made a guest appearance here. Among some of the most famous events to be held at Madison Square Garden were the legendary boxing matches between Joe Frazier and Muhammad Ali, the Concert for New York City after the attacks of September 11, George Harrison's epic Concert for Bangladesh, and John Lennon's last concert before his murder in 1980. The plain building complex contains a stadium that seats 20,000 people and a function room that holds 1,000. There are also exhibition rooms, restaurants, malls and even a cinema on the site.

The destruction of the old Pennsylvania Station was a prerequisite for this project, and it raised the ire of preservationists, but to appear once in Madison Square Garden is the dream not only of musicians but of athletes as well. Below left: A super-bantamweight boxing match between Lante Addy and Jorge Diaz. Below: Kobe Bryant of the Los Angeles Lakers after a successful dunk against the New York Knicks.

EMPIRE STATE BUILDING

Since the destruction of the World Trade Center towers, the Empire State Building is once again New York's tallest building at 381 m (1,250 ft) in height – 449 m (1,473 ft) including the radio mast. As many as 34,000 workers, including many Native Americans from the Mohawk Nation, were employed at peak times during the building's construction. Designed by architects Schreve, Lamb & Harmon, it was opened on May 1, 1931 when President Herbert Hoover pressed a button in the White House in Washington to turn on the lights in the building in Manhattan. Officially, there are 102 floors, but only 85 of these contain office space that can be rented. On the 86th floor of the building there is a viewing platform and at the top is a dome originally intended as a mooring-place for airships; this plan had to be abandoned, however, due to the dangerous updraughts.

At night, the illuminated Empire State Building is an impressive sight (below). The floodlights are turned off only during bird migrations to prevent the birds from crashing into the building. On national holidays the upper floors are lit red, white and blue. Visitors are greeted by the brilliant marble and chrome Art Deco lobby (far left). Left: The observation deck on the 86th floor at 320 m (1,050 ft) above the street.

SKYSCRAPERS AND SKYWALKERS

New York's skyscrapers were never the oldest (those were built in Chicago in 1880), nor are they any longer the tallest (nowadays these are scattered around Asia), but among them there are some of the most beautiful (the Chrysler Building) and certainly the most famous (the Empire State Building). Their construction was made possible with the development of resilient types of steel and safe elevators. Their load-bearing structure invariably consisted of a frame, which was generally one of two types: either a "skeleton frame" or a cantilevered frame. In the first instance, a frame mostly constructed from stable steel columns and beams supports all the walls and floors; in the second, the main support is a central concrete column housing the elevator and utility shafts and from which the floors are suspended. The Empire State Building was one of the last steel-framed building projects to be completed with riveted steel beams before more reliable welded joints replaced this technique. The construction of New York's skyscrapers is impossible to imagine without the aid of the Mohawk iron workers – Native American construction workers who were known as "skywalkers" for their agility and their ability to balance on vertiginous steel beams that were sometimes only 15 cm (6 inches) across.

The steel beams on which workers had to make their way during the construction of a skyscraper were sometimes only 15 cm (6 in) wide (below). The framework of the Flatiron Building (left) was also put up as a steel skeleton, which is characteristic of a skyscraper. Only after this is complete is the building filled out with cement to form walls and floors; this type of construction ensures the stability of the structure.

THE MORGAN LIBRARY & MUSEUM

John Pierpont Morgan (1837–1913) was born in Hartford, Connecticut, the son of a successful banker and financier. After a stint in Europe, J.P. returned to New York to forge his own way and in 1860 founded J.P. Morgan & Co. In addition to his business accumen, he was also one of the greatest collectors of rare books and original manuscripts of his time. Between 1903 and 1906 he had architects McKim, Mead & White design a magnificent build-ing for the garden behind his house on Park Avenue and Madison Avenue, where his collection of treasures including rare manuscripts, books and prints can still be seen today. At the beginning of the twentieth century, the structure was completely remodeled by Renzo Piano and a four-story building was added. In 2005, it was renamed the Morgan Library & Museum and since 2006 the entire complex has once again been open to the public.

Among the treasures belonging to John Pierpont Morgan's collections are valuable manuscripts and incunabula – printed books from the first decades of the printing press. Below left: The library interior. Below right: An illustration of a French bible. Left: The main building on the corner of Madison Avenue and 37th Street, a National Historic Landmark since 1966 that was designed by Renzo Piano.

NEW YORK PUBLIC LIBRARY, BRYANT PARK

New York Public Library is one of the world's greatest libraries, housing some 49.5 million archived documents including more than eighteen million books. It occupies a monumental Beaux Arts building made of elegant marble located on Fifth Avenue that was designed by architects Carrère & Hastings in 1911. The entrance to the library is guarded by two stone lions. Prior to its construction, the site was home to a potter's field and later a drinking water reservoir for the city. Among the valuable treasures kept in the library are the Gutenberg Bible, a letter from Christopher Columbus and a handwritten draft of the Declaration of Independence penned by Thomas Jefferson himself. Bryant Park, which adjoins the western end of the library, is also worth a visit, especially during warmer months when the film festival takes place there.

The enormous main reading room of the New York Public Library stretches over two blocks and can sit five hundred readers. Items stored in underground rooms are brought up surprisingly quickly to library members – anybody who lives, works, or attends school in New York can apply for a library card. Classic movies are often shown outside in summer in Bryant Park (left).

GRAND CENTRAL TERMINAL

Built in the Beaux Arts style and decorated with baroque and Renaissance elements, Grand Central Terminal opened in its current form in 1913 after several years of construction. It is still the largest and busiest rail station in the world. A Roman triumphal arch provides an orientation point at the entrance on East 42nd Street while Corinthian columns support the giant arched windows and a bronze statue commemorates Cornelius Vander-bilt, the railroad magnate. Known as the "Commodore", Vanderbilt combined his railroad services to create the "New York Central System". It was his grandson who built the station. A roof decorated with stars arches over a flagstone floor in the magnificent main hall, twelve floors high and meant to resemble Roman baths. Referred to as Grand Central by New Yorkers, the station is used by more than 125,000 commuters a day.

The "heavenly vaulted" main hall of Grand Central Station (below) vibrates with activity. The main entrance on East 42nd Street (other images) is crowned by three sculptures representing Mercury, Hercules and Minerva. You can do more than just catch a train when you visit the station. In fact, you'll find the Grand Central Oyster Bar here, which boasts "the freshest seafood in Manhattan".

CHRYSLER BUILDING

Built in 1930, the Chrysler Building was not just intended as office space for the car firm of the same name, but also as a memorial for its owner, Walter P. Chrysler, whose career had begun on the shop floor of the Union Pacific Railroad. "His" skyscraper was to rise as steeply into the New York sky as his career had risen when he moved into the car industry, and it was also to be the most beautiful and the tallest building in the city. Most New Yorkers would agree that his architect, William Van Alen, succeeded in his aesthetic pursuits. Regarding height, Van Alen found himself in a battle with his former partner, H. Craig Severance, who was planning the tallest building in the world for the Bank of Manhattan Company. At 319 m (1,046 ft), the Chrysler Building ended up victorious, but the glory only lasted a year until it was overtaken by the Empire State Building.

The stainless steel exterior on the crown of the Chrysler Building recalls an automobile radiator. In the race to put up the tallest building in the world, architects used a variety of tricks – in this case, assembling the 55.5 m (180 ft) spire in a ventilation shaft before putting it in place to complete the building. At 319 m (1,046 ft), they achieved their goal, but were outdone the next year by the Empire State Building.

CITY LIGHTS – AFTER HOURS

It was certainly not by accident that Charlie Chaplin chose New York as the setting for his last silent film, *City Lights* (1931). Where could he have found a better backdrop than here, among the glittering skyscrapers of Manhattan, for his romantic fairy tale about the tramp who falls in love with a blind flower seller? The city that never sleeps has always been an ideal landscape for filmmakers to capture and project their fantasies and desires. Perhaps the most beautiful homage to the city, and one that also evokes the nocturnal atmosphere, is Woody Allen's *Manhattan* (1979), while Martin Scorsese in his film *After Hours* (1985) succeeds in showing the city at night almost bursting with energy. Brian De Palma, in *The Bonfire of the Vanities* (1987), his film adaptation of Tom Wolfe's novel, tells of how dangerous it was to take the wrong highway exit in New York in the 1980s. In his 1991 novel *American Psycho* (adapted for the screen in 2000), Bret Easton Ellis paints the monstrous nightmare world of a Wall Street yuppie gone mad. But it was Charlie Chaplin who discovered – or created – the cinematic model that still holds true for this city: the romantic fable where, for example, a poor vagrant can find love in a blind flower seller.

Manhattan's skyline is the defining image of a modern – and post-modern – city. "It was unbelievable; the city showed itself gigantic, confusing, inexplicable, and beautiful in its distant, smoking reality, with dazzling rows of windows and canyons. A pink light was shining over the tallest peaks, while bottomless shadows hung in the massive chasms," wrote Jack Kerouac.

570 LEXINGTON AVENUE

One of New York's most complete Art Deco creations is this strikingly beautiful building on Lexington Avenue. Originally built to a design by the Cross & Cross practice for the broadcasters RCA ("Radio Corporation of America"), it later became the headquarters of the General Electric power company. The historic building – not to be confused with the GE (General Electric) Building in the Rockefeller Center – makes interesting architectural references to St Bartholomew's Church, which stands beside it. When the office block was constructed, the materials used – brick, aluminium and stone – were chosen in order to harmonize with the church, while the rear elevation of the General Electric building was styled partly to form a backdrop to it. The architectural harmony is visually stunning and the building certainly ranks amongst New York's finest examples of Art Deco design.

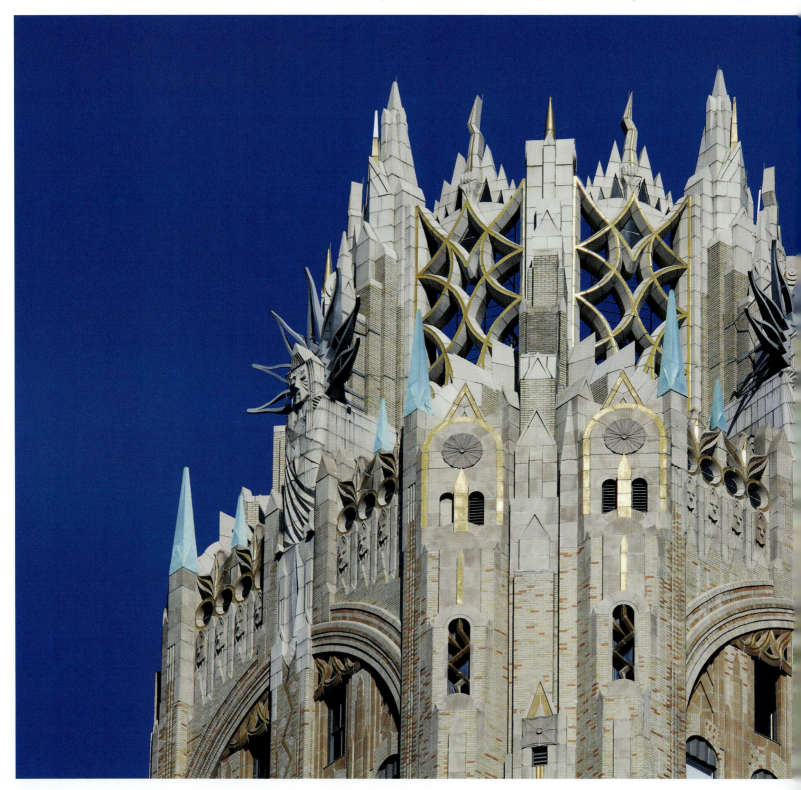

The Art Deco crown of this building symbolizes radio waves, a reference to the radio company which commissioned it – RCA. After the company moved to Rockefeller Center in 1931, the original "RCA Victor Building" was renamed the "General Electric Building". Art Deco elements are also found in the lobby area. The clock on the façade still sports the initials "GE" for General Electric.

UNITED NATIONS HEADQUARTERS

The Headquarters of the United Nations (UN) is located on what is considered international soil on the banks of the East River. It is the site of a former slaughterhouse district. John D. Rockefeller Jr was originally the owner of the land and later donated it to the United Nations. The USA provided an interest-free loan of $67 million for the building, and between 1947 and 1950 the simple tower that houses the UN Secretary-General's office was constructed based on designs by an international committee of renowned architects that included Le Corbusier, Oscar Niemeyer and Sven Markelius, to name but a few. The General Assembly Building, which is used as an auditorium, was added later along with the Conference Building and the Dag Hamarskjöld Library. The gardens and the lobby of the General Assembly Building are open to the public and the other buildings are accessible on guided tours.

The General Assembly (below, with President Barack Obama at the speaker's desk) meets every year in September to discuss and approve the budget for the United Nations. The most powerful organ of the UN is the Security Council (left, the council chamber with a mural by Per Krogh depicting a phoenix rising from the ashes, symbolizing the world after World War II).

TRUMP WORLD TOWER

Real estate tycoon Donald Trump isn't the only one who enjoys a comfortable home with an unobstructed view of the city. Don't worry – there are still a few units for sale in Trump World Tower, one of the tallest apartment buildings in the world. Built between 1999 and 2001 it rises 262 m (861 ft) over the East River on United Nations Plaza. "Apartments" would be the wrong word to use here – one speaks of "residences", and the term "high price" should be taken at face value, as it were. Although there are "studios" (with bathroom, no bedrooms) for the smaller budget – a mere 875,000 dollars for slightly more than 50 sq m (540 sq ft) – the upper categories are far more interesting. How about approximately 500 sq m (5,400 sq ft) with seven bathrooms and six bedrooms for reasonable $12,400,000? That's a bargain anywhere!

The truly expensive residences in the Trump World Tower have long been sold, and the people who live here – such as Sophia Loren – are also not fussed that from the outside this black monolith designed by Greek architect Costas Condylis directly across from the United Nations is no beauty. After all, it's what's inside that counts.

PARK AVENUE

The New York and Harlem Railroad was one of the first private rail companies in the United States, and also probably the first one to operate streetcars from Lower Manhattan to Harlem. Starting in the 1830s, its tracks ran along the street originally named "Fourth Avenue". In the 1860s, the section between 34th and 40th Streets was renamed Park Avenue (the rails here ran through the then upper-class neighborhood of Murray Hill, which had green areas somewhat reminiscent of a park). Today, the entire course of the street between Union Square and the Harlem River is called Park Avenue but the tracks were placed underground a long time ago and now run north as part of Metro-North Railroad's Harlem Line. Above ground, Park Avenue developed into one of the most desirable and expensive areas in town, especially in the section between 42nd and 59th Streets.

The middle portion of Park Avenue forms a ribbon cutting through midtown Manhattan (far left) where more offices (with nearly three million jobs) and hotels are clustered than in any other comparable space. Some of the skyscrapers here have made architectural history (below, the Mutual of America Building at 320 Park Avenue, and left, the Helmsley Building, 230 Park Avenue).

WALDORF-ASTORIA HOTEL

Designed by Schultze & Weaver, this legendary hotel on Park Avenue opened for business in 1931 and is one of the city's most fascinating Art Deco buildings. You can still play Cole Porter's piano, which stands in the lobby. Now officially marketed under the name "Waldorf=Astoria", with two dashes, it originally had one hyphen as it had been two hotels with a connecting corridor. "Meet me at The Hyphen" became a popular song and expression at the time, with the word "hyphen" used to refer to the hotel, but the name did not stick. William Waldorf Astor built the original 13-floor Waldorf Hotel in 1893, and four years later his cousin, John Jacob Astor, built the Astoria, which was four floors higher, right next door. Construction work on the Empire State Building meant that the building had to close. When the new hotel was built, the name was changed to Waldorf-Astoria.

The Waldorf-Astoria (far left and below, the entrance on Park Avenue) was the largest hotel in the world when it opened its doors on October 1, 1931. The lobby (left) features a large clock originally built for the Chicago World's Fair of 1893 that previously graced the old Waldorf-Astoria on Fifth Avenue. Since 1935, the "International Debutante's Ball" has been held every year in December in the hotel's three-story ballroom.

ST PATRICK'S CATHEDRAL

In 1828, the Roman Catholic Church in New York bought a parcel of land outside the city limits for use as a cemetery. In 1850, after the undersoil had proved too stony for such a purpose, Archbishop John Hughes decided to commission a cathedral along European lines for this location on Fifth Avenue. Eight years later, work began on a neo-Gothic cathedral designed by architect James Renwick; it was completed in 1879. In 1910, it was dedicated to St Patrick, the patron saint of Ireland. A statue within its walls commemorates Elizabeth Ann Seton (1774–1821), the founder of the order of the Sisters of Charity and the first American citizen to be canonized. St Patrick's Cathedral, which can seat 2,500, is the see of the archbishop of New York. Over five million people per year come to the cathedral to visit or pray. If you have time, try to attend an organ mass here.

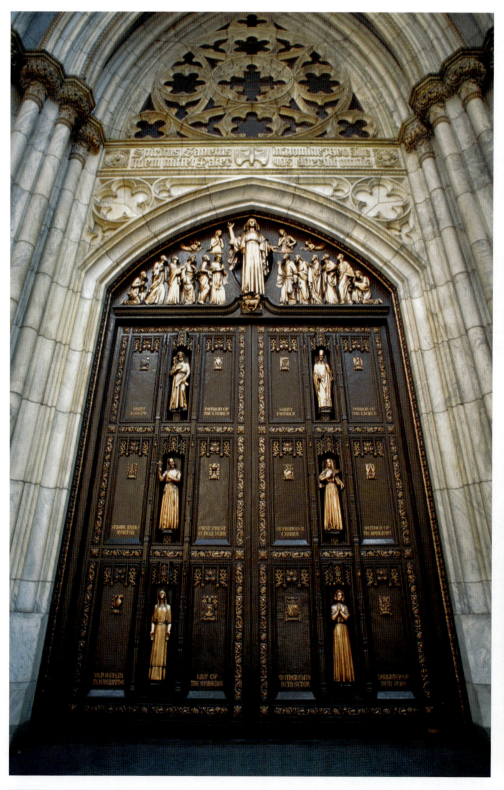

Atlas bears the world on his shoulders, while the Catholic church provides spiritual guidance (left). It's hard to imagine that the 101 m (330 ft) towers weren't added until nine years after the completion of the impressive structure. The massive bronze doors, decorated with sacred figures from the city of New York (below, left) weigh nine tons. Inside, massive marble columns support the vaulted ceiling (below).

CITYGROUP CENTER, LIPSTICK, SONY TOWER

The Citigroup Center (formerly Citicorp Center) was designed by Hugh Stubbins & Associates – now called KlingStubbins – and built in 1977 on four nine-floor stilts. Interestingly, the stilts were not placed at the corners of the rectangular building, but were instead situated in the middle of each side. This was because trustees of St Peter's Church would only sell part of their land and property rights on the sole condition that they would be allowed to construct a new church "under" the skyscraper. This now stands beneath the extended north-west corner of the Citigroup Center. The "Sony Building", located on Madison Avenue, was built in 1984 for communications company AT&T, and is now called the Sony Building after a change of ownership. Designed by Philip Johnson, his unusual and individual design for the "world's first post-modern skyscraper" continues to cause controversy and divide opinion.

The slanted roof of the Citigroup Center (below) was intended to bear solar panels, a plan that was never realized. With its elliptical ground plan, the high-rise building that is officially named after its address, 53rd at Third, is popularly known as the "Lipstick" building (below left). The Sony tower (left) is also known as the "Chippendale Building" because its gabled roof recalls the English furniture style.

BROADWAY

Called the "Great White Way" for the many lights along the theater section, Broadway is quite possibly the most famous street in the world. Nik Cohn, an English journalist and author of an article that formed the basis for the film *Saturday Night Fever*, referred to this microcosm as the "heart of the world". Despite the fact that his article turned out to be fabricated, the street certainly has the potential to provide plenty of inspiration. The best way to discover the myths and mysteries, however, is to walk down this legendary avenue yourself. In reality, Broadway is a diagonal road that cuts across the grid of the city from Bowling Green downtown through all of Manhattan and on up to the Bronx. The mythical portion of the street is still alive and well, primarily in the section between 41st and 53rd Streets, which is where Times Square is located.

Originally, journalist Nik Cohn wanted to travel around the world, but then he realized that "if you only just walked down a block of Broadway, you'd discover a hundred worlds." So he started on his way, and many followed him (left). On 34th Street and Broadway you'll find Macy's flagship store, the biggest department store in the world, with 198,500 sq m (2,136,000 sq ft) of floor space (below).

SHOWTIME: LIVE ON BROADWAY

If show business has a birthplace, it is to be found in New York. Even during the initial waves of immigration, theater performances were considered a very welcome escape from the trials of an often grim daily life. The theater was like a second home for many, not least because the plays were frequently performed in their native languages. Initially, there were only amateur performances, the first professional production of Shakespeare's *Richard III* having taken place at the New Theater in Nassau Street in 1750. The 19th century was the great era of vaudeville shows, which combined drama, music, comedy and circus acts. The start of the 20th century saw the dawning of the real age of Broadway as more and more theaters moved into the area around Times Square, the center of New York nightlife at the time. The Empire Theater moved from Herald Square to Broadway in 1893, and from then until 1930 many more theaters such as the New Lyceum opened their doors. After a short crisis in the 1980s, spectacular musicals including *Cats*, *Phantom of the Opera* and *Lion King* continued the earlier successes. Nowadays, there are about forty large theaters and a number of smaller ones active on Broadway. Catching a show here during a trip to New York is a memorable experience.

Broadway leads from the Battery in southern Manhattan to Yonkers and Albany in upstate New York. It is the most vigorous artery to break through the checkerboard layout that prevails elsewhere in the city. Broadway forms a vast diagonal as it cuts its way through the concrete jungle, reaching its glittering high point around Times Square in the sea of lights of the Broadway shows.

TIMES SQUARE

You can still hear the heartbeat of New York on Times Square, but the city's former fleshpots have been transformed into a more sterile consumer affair à la Disneyworld. The mighty shopping malls and themed restaurants now set the tone in an area that was once notorious for its seamy side. The pickpockets, drug dealers and prostitutes have moved on and the XXX-rated posters, porn stores and peepshows are now all but forgotten.

In 1900, this was still a rural area called Longacre Square, used primarily as a storage area with stables and barns. It was not named Times Square until 1904, in honor of the long-respected newspaper the New York Times, which was building a giant office block there. Events from all over the world have flashed across the famous newsticker on the façade since 1928, but these days the paper is edited from Eighth Avenue offices.

Except for Seventh Avenue – the only road
that is still a thoroughfare – Times Square was
transformed into a pedestrian zone in 2009. As
a comparison, our photo on the foldout pages
shows the situation before the change; the other
photos were taken after the completion of the
"traffic-free area". For New York's taxi drivers
it is still a bone of contention, but most people
are getting used to the new situation.

HOT DOGS ON EVERY CORNER

All you need to do is heat up a couple of simple knackwurst-style sausages – wieners or frankfurters will do – put them in a soft, plain bun and then pile on the toppings: ketchup and mustard go without saying, onions, beef chili if you're feeling adventurous, and lots of relish. True connoisseurs also appreciate a dollop of sauerkraut as an addition to this tasty morsel. And presto! Dinner is served! In New York, hot dogs can be bought at just about every street corner – not just around Times Square. Add a soda and a "hot pretzel" if you're going for the whole dining experience. They are supposed to have been invented by a Polish immigrant called Nathan Handwerker, who opened his first hot dog stall in 1916 on Coney Island. It is common knowledge, however, that behind every great man stands an even greater woman, and in this case it was from his wife Ida that Nathan learned the secret recipe. Since then, the stall has become a restaurant chain that specializes in hot dogs and is so well known that its renown is even part of its name: "Nathan's Famous". A yearly contest that takes place in its Coney Island branch may have contributed to the chain's fame: the contestants eat as many hot dogs as they can in ten minutes. In order to stand a chance of winning, you will need to manage more than fifty.

HOT DOGS ON EVERY CORNER

Hot dogs come in a wide variety of shapes and sizes, but nobody knows for sure where the name for this "typical American" treat came from. Perhaps it really is linked to the caricaturist Tad Dorgan who is said to have been annoyed by the barking of dogs during a baseball game at Polo Grounds, as a result of which he drew one of the yapping creatures between two halves of a bun and wrote "hot dog" underneath.

AVENUE OF THE AMERICAS (SIXTH AVENUE)

Sixth Avenue leads from Little Italy in southern Manhattan to Central Park South. Mayor Fiorello La Guardia changed its name to "Avenue of the Americas" in 1945, but the new name never really caught on. Since the 1980s, both names are shown on signs. It also came to be known as "Fashion Road" because of all the shops that opened towards the end of the 19th century between 14th Street and Herald Square. The rail tracks of the Sixth Avenue Elevated overshadowed the road until 1939, but once the railway had been put out of service and replaced with the IND Sixth Avenue subway, a series of tall office blocks were built along the street. One example is the 38-story CBS Building, which is home to the Columbia Broadcasting System media company. Completed in 1965, the headquarters are also known as "Black Rock" because of its dark granite exterior.

There are virtually no reminders of the turn of the 20th century, when New York's upper-class ladies went to Broadway by horse carriage. Now it's all modern buildings made of glass. But back then, they shopped in the elegant stores along "Ladies Mile" – between 18th and 23rd Street – while the middle classes bought their goods on the same avenue a few blocks away in what was called "Fashion Road".

NEW YORK FASHION: RUNWAYS, RAGS AND RICHES

The hottest shows in town are definitely not confined to Broadway. Not if you're talking about fashion, anyway. New York Fashion Week takes place twice a year, once in February and once again in September. Celebrity stars like Natalie Portman and Chloë Sevigny get to sit in the front row, right next to the runway, as trendy fashion labels like Rodarte and Tibi and established houses from Donna Karan and Diane von Furstenberg to Ralph Lauren, Calvin Klein and Marc Jacobs present their latest collections. Fashion Week was originally conceived by fashion journalist Eleanor Lambert as "Press Week" in 1943, and was the world's first organized seven-day-long fashion event. Initially, the aim was to draw attention away from the fact that the typical trips to Paris fashion shows were no longer possible during the war. Its success proved sustainable. Today, it is one of the most important fashion weeks in the world along with London, Milan and Paris. Since 1994, the shows have been held in large white tents in Bryant Park (which borders Sixth Avenue at 40th Street), and the event has been rebranded "Mercedes-Benz Fashion Week" since 2009. In 2010, the New York-based event sponsored by the German luxury brand moved to Damrosch Park at the Lincoln Center.

A great deal of money, and even more influence, is at stake at the biannual New York Fashion Week. If the clothes showcased by the models on the runways find favor with the fashion editors of Vogue & co., the haute couture (below left, Australian label Willow; below, New York label Philip Lim) created specially for the shows is made into prêt-à-porter clothes – clothes that are "ready to be worn".

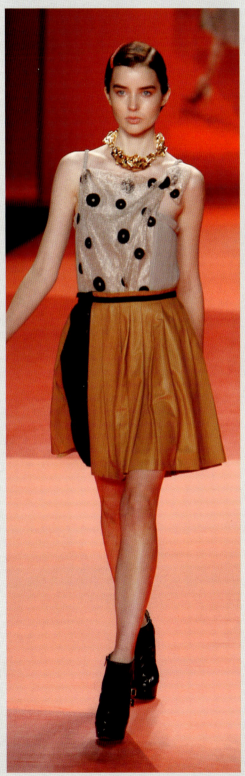

FIFTH AVENUE

Dividing Manhattan virtually down the middle, Fifth Avenue begins at Washington Square in Greenwich Village, crosses Midtown, passes Central Park, and runs along the Upper East Side to the Harlem River. In the second half of the 19th century, affluent families – the Astors, Forbes, Fricks, Rockefellers, Vanderbilts, and others – sought to escape cramped southern Manhattan and built their villas along Fifth Avenue's first few miles, bringing it the nickname of "Millionaires' Row". By the beginning of the 20th century, more and more businesses had moved in, causing the rich – who today mostly live around Central Park – to move even further uptown. Now flagship stores from famous brands such as Armani, Cartier, Chanel, Escada, Prada, Tiffany and Versace draw crowds of visitors. It doesn't get much better than this for those who enjoy a little retail therapy.

A world of exclusive goods awaits on Fifth Avenue, which runs from north to south through the skyscraper chasms of Manhattan. The most talked-about section lies between 48th and 59th Street where the highest concentration of the most expensive and elegant shops associated with Fifth Avenue are located. The Apple Store here (767 Fifth Avenue) is open 24 hours a day, 365 days a year.

ROCKEFELLER CENTER

This gigantic complex of skyscrapers between 47th and 50th Streets was built in the 1930s for John D. Rockefeller Jr by a select team of architects led by Raymond Hood. The complex has since been expanded several times and houses offices, TV studios, restaurants and stores. Built in 1933 to a height of 260 m (853 ft), the GE (General Electric) Building is at the heart of the complex. Its viewing platform, "Top of the Rock", offers a magnificent view of the city's skyline. The GE Building is also home to broadcaster NBC, whose legendary Today Show – the oldest factual television show, first screened on 14 January 1952 – is broadcast every morning from 7.00 till 9.00 from a glass studio in the GE Building. Less well-known but equally fascinating is the underground concourse, home to retail stores, fast food outlets and other venues. It's New York's largest underground city.

The Rockefeller Center (left, the Rockefeller Plaza, guarded by Paul Manship's *Prometheus* statue and converted into an ice rink in the winter) is the largest complex of its kind in private ownership. It belongs to the real estate company Tishman Speyer. The central building is the GE (General Electric) Building (bottom left). The Atlas statue (below) was created by Lee Lawrie and Rene Paul Chambellan in 1937.

TOP OF THE ROCK

Would you like to see Manhattan through the eyes of John D. Rockefeller Jr? The "Top of the Rock" makes it possible. This is the name given to the observation deck on top of the GE (General Electric) Building. It actually comprises three floors – the 67th, 69th and 70th – the latter of which is the top floor of the highest skyscraper of the Rockefeller Center. It is simultaneously the most interesting vantage point for photographers: the terrace provides the only truly unobstructed view of surrounding Midtown Manhattan, while the other two floors are still enclosed by panorama windows. The observation deck was closed for almost 20 years before being reopened, following a renovation that cost $75 million and was completed on November 1, 2005 – "for the world to see Manhattan the way he [Rockefeller] imagined it".

The breathtaking panorama views of the surrounding skyscrapers from the observation deck of the GE (General Electric) Building is rivaled only by that of the observation decks of the 86th and 102nd floor of the Empire State Building. The only obvious difference is that you can't see the Empire State Building from the Empire State Building, but you can from the Top of the Rock.

ART DÉCO: DECORATIVE ART IN ARCHITECTURE

Art Deco is a term describing one of the more imaginative, whimsical and indeed artistic movements of the 1920s and 1930s. The name originally came from a crafts exhibition (the "Exposition Internationale des Arts Decoratifs et Industriels Modernes") which was held in Paris in 1925 and soon attracted interest across the Atlantic. Developed as a counter to what were regarded as the excesses of art nouveau, the style influenced every branch of art and design as well as fashion, furniture and architecture. The designs were typified by sleek, streamlined forms and geometric patterns created by artists who plundered a rich diversity of historic sources for their work. This fusion of modernity and history produced opulent and lavish designs created from both valuable and new materials such as marble, granite, steel, chrome and bakelite and combined with bold tonal schemes. In the explosive boom years of early high-rise construction, Art Deco offered New York's architects all kinds of new possibilities: artistic decoration outshone mere functionality while streamlining the skyscrapers' block-like appearance and bringing a playful element to the city's otherwise rather sober building styles. Art Deco buildings are today considered some of the city's most stunning constructions.

ART DÉCO: DECORATIVE ART IN ARCHITECTURE

The Rockefeller Center is one of New York's Art Deco jewels and its foyers and gardens feature works by roughly thirty artists. Below: Lee Lawrie's *Wisdom* relief at the main entrance of the GE Building. Below left: *The Joy of Life* by Attilio Piccirilli (1937, 1 Rockefeller Plaza). Left: *Dance, Drama, and Song* by Hildreth Meiere (1932, Radio City Music Hall).

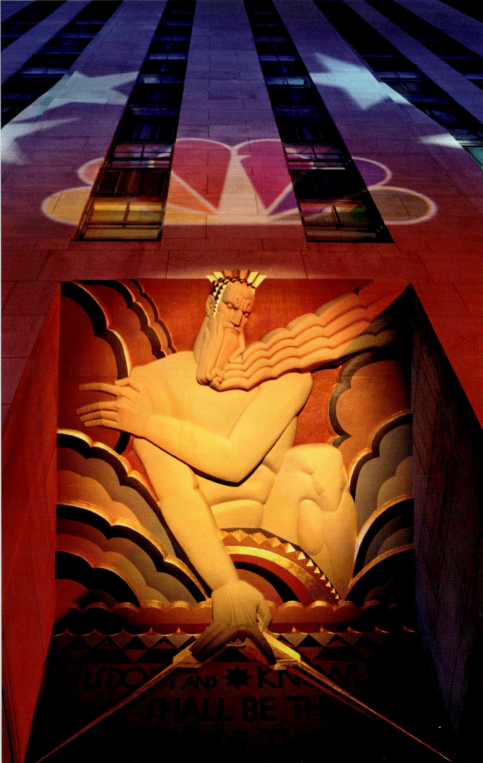

RADIO CITY MUSIC HALL

Radio City Music Hall, which is part of the Rockefeller Center, is historicly the "showplace of the nation". Designed by architect Edward Durell for impresario Samuel "Roxy" Rothafel, who found fame and fortune during the silent film era, this entertainment complex opened on December 27, 1932 and has since received more than 300 million visitors from around the world. Originally intended as a variety hall, the 6,200-seat audito-rium was soon refurbished as a cinema that could also host stage productions. The dance troupe, the Rockettes, became legendary, and in various formations also took part in the traditional annual Christmas shows that began in 1933. Nowadays, Radio City Music Hall is best known as a live venue for rock and pop stars. The two remaining Beatles, Paul McCartney and Ringo Starr, performed here at a charity concert on April 4, 2009.

Just before 2000, Radio City Music Hall, a protected historical monument, underwent the most comprehensive renovations in its history. More than $70 million were invested to retain its historical ambience while integrating the most up-to-date technology. Performances at the MTV Video Music Awards by pop icons such as Christina Aguilera, Madonna and Britney Spears have become the stuff of legends.

SOUNDTRACK OF THE CITY: SINATRA'S "NEW YORK, NEW YORK"

"Start spreading the news / I am leaving today / I want to be a part of it / New York, New York..." This song made world-famous by Liza Minnelli and Frank Sinatra quickly became the unofficial soundtrack of the city. The song, whose full title is *Theme from New York, New York*, was composed by Fred Ebb and John Kander. It was the title song of the eponymous musical film that opened in cinemas in 1977 and was nominated for four Golden Globes. Liza Minnelli and Robert De Niro played the leading parts, and it was directed by Martin Scorsese. The film is about a musician and a singer who marry after the end of World War II and have to sacrifice their love to their careers. *New York, New York*, an enthusiastic declaration of love to the "city that never sleeps", is sung at the end of the film by Liza Minnelli. Both Liza Minnelli and Frank Sinatra incorporated the song into their concert repertoires, turning it into something of a hymn. Sinatra released it as a single in March 1980, and there are several recordings of live performances by both of them. The song is often confused with another song entitled *New York, New York* by Leonard Bernstein, Betty Comden and Adolph Green. This features in the musical *On the Town* and was also sung by Frank Sinatra. This declaration of love to the metropolis also became a sort of hymn.

Francis Albert Sinatra (1915–1998) was born the son of Italian immigrants in Hoboken, New Jersey. He sang in the big bands of Harry James and Tommy Dorsey, earning the nickname "The Voice". He landed a number of hits, and was rewarded with full houses in New York and beyond. Even for contemporary rappers (left), Sinatra's interpretation of *My Way* has become an anthem of sorts.

ALL THINGS EXPENSIVE AND BEAUTIFUL: SHOPPING IN NEW YORK

New York is shopping heaven. Countless stores and outlets offer everything the retail heart could desire, from sinfully expensive designer clothes to cheap jeans. Macy's, for example, the biggest department store in the world, is split between two buildings and has a sales floor of no less than 200,000 sq m (2.1 million sq ft) spread over ten floors. Bloomingdale's sells smart designer fashion at sometimes surprisingly affordable prices, while Lord & Taylor's in the Empire State Building has classic upmarket styles. Diamond Row, between 40th and 50th Streets, is so named for the glittering jewels on display. Amongst the most popular stores on Fifth Avenue are Tiffany & Co., Prada and Versace while FAO Schwarz toy store is not just for little ones. Antiques, art, and fashion can be found in the trendier districts of SoHo and TriBeCa, and Greenwich Village is famous for its offbeat and alternative stores that are ideal for books, records, CDs and esoteric odds and ends. There are also specialist shops for gays and lesbians in a number of places. Discount stores have congregated on Herald Square, in the shadow of Macy's, and you can buy reasonably priced fashion, bags and shoes on Historic Orchard Street in the East Village. You really can shop till you drop as there is something new around every corner.

ALL THINGS EXPENSIVE AND BEAUTIFUL: SHOPPING IN NEW YORK

The window displays of Saks (left), Sisley (below left) and Victoria's Secret (below) on Fifth Avenue are truly seductive. Given the wide variety of goods on offer, it is no wonder we are tempted to spend our hard-earned cash.

MUSEUM OF MODERN ART (MOMA)

All it took was three friends, and in a case of pure girl power, the Museum of Modern Art (MoMA) was founded in 1929 by Mary Quinn Sullivan, Abby Aldrich Rockefeller and Lillie P. Bliss, although the museum's official history still oddly refers to the first two as Mrs Cornelius J. Sullivan and Mrs John D. Rockefeller Jr – only Lillie, who never married, is credited under her own first name. Known as "the ladies", "the daring ladies", or "the adaman-tine ladies", all three were proven patrons of the arts (and artists) and decided to find a common home for their passion and their collections. The museum opened its doors on November 7, 1929, and the ladies enlisted art historian Alfred H. Barr as its director. It moved location several times before finally ending up at its current site. It was built in 1939 according to designs by architects Philip Goodwin and Edward Durell.

From its inception, MoMA was to be "the greatest museum of modern art in the world" (Alfred H. Barr, Jr). Its collection contains pop-art classics such as Warhol's *Campbell's Soup* (1962, below left) as well as Monet's *Water Lilies* (ca. 1920, below). By 2004, the area available for exhibitions and other museum activities had been virtually doubled and now comprises approximately 58,000 sq m (625,000 sq ft).

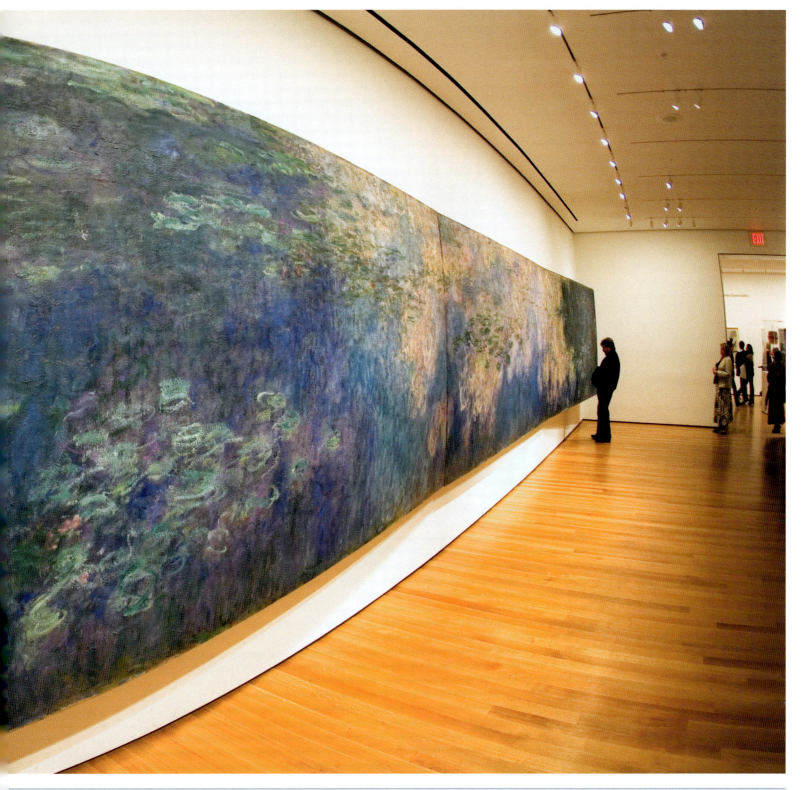

TRUMP TOWER

Few find it beautiful, but most want to have seen it: Trump Tower at the corner of Fifth Avenue and 56th Street. It was built according to plans by Der Scutt of Swanke Hayden Connell and officially completed on November 30, 1983. At a height of 202 m (666 ft) with sixty-eight stories, the glass palace is symbolic of the rise of property tycoon Donald Trump, who created an urban memorial to himself in this way. The Trump International Hotel and Tower on Central Park had opened in 1971, and in 2001, the New York portfolio was extended to include the Trump World Tower at the United Nations, but none of these buildings made him as well known as Trump Tower. The latter's entrance area on Fifth Avenue is decorated with two free-standing golden Ts. The color scheme inside the glass palace is also dominated by lots of gold and much less silver.

The six-story-high atrium (left) is the main attraction of Trump Tower (below, the entrance on Fifth Avenue, and far left, an employee in front of the entrance). Its walls and floor are made of Italian marble whose color palette goes well with the golden escalators. Below left: James Carpenter and Friday Giannini (Gucci Creative Director) designed Gucci's largest flagship store over three floors of Trump Tower.

GRAND ARMY PLAZA, PLAZA HOTEL

Fifth Avenue comes to a grand end at Grand Army Plaza by Central Park, at the south-east corner of which horse-drawn buggies begin their relaxing trips through the city. Built in 1915, the Pulitzer fountain in the middle commemorates the famous publisher and the plaza's northern half boasts an equestrian statue of William Tecumseh Sherman, the Civil War General. Built by Henry J. Hardenberg in 1907 in the style of a French chateau, the legendary Plaza hotel was once advertised with the slogan "Nothing boring ever happens at the Plaza". Some $400 million was spent on restorations between 2005 and 2007, and the slogan still applies. Today, the site is no longer "just" a hotel. Some of the area has now been turned over for private homes, with stores, bars and restaurants that are open to the public.

Few can afford a night at the Plaza Hotel (left, with the equestrian statue of the Civil War General William Tecumseh Sherman in the foreground and below, the entrance) located at the gracefully designed Grand Army Plaza. For those who can't, there is always afternoon tea in the Palm Court. Below: High society celebrates itself at debutante balls where a lot of money is donated to charity.

VANISHING POINT OF DREAMS AND ASPIRATIONS: NEW YORK'S SKYLINE

"Whether you're in a snack bar in Manila, an ice-cream parlour in Munich or an office complex in Moscow," writes journalist, columnist and author Andrian Kreye in his book *Broadway Ecke Canal* (in German), "somewhere or other you will always find a picture of the New York skyline as a newspaper clipping, a postcard or a framed print. And everywhere it seems to serve as a focal point for dreams and aspirations." It was so, it is so and it will probably always be so. Maybe we should imagine the New York skyline as an aging diva who has lost nothing of her grandezza. As she stands there before us, always elegant and yet slightly vulnerable at the same time, she perhaps shows us not only the countenance of this magnificent city, but also the countenance of an era as it inexorably marches onward and finally vanishes from sight.

VANISHING POINT FOR DREAMS AND ASPIRATIONS: NEW YORK'S SKYLINE

"Here, they had New York. The silhouettes of the buildings, the towers of New York, floated like icons over the landscape and represented everything that was great, glorious and triumphant about New York ... It was as though one were in a transparent Easter egg with an artificial landscape, and the towers of New York stood there like a vanishing cameo background."
(Tom Wolfe)

CARNEGIE HALL

Perhaps it was a good omen that the architect of Carnegie Hall, William B. Tuthill, not only had a fondness for music, but also played the cello himself. In any case, the venue was built in 1890 and 1891 according to his designs for millionaire steel tycoon Andrew Carnegie and continues to be one of the most famous concert halls in the world. This is largely due to its terrific acoustics, for which Tuthill created the ideal architectural space. The acoustics were first praised in May 1891, when Carnegie Hall was inaugurated with a five-day-long festival at which Russian composer Peter Tchaikovsky acted as guest conductor. Carnegie Hall should really be called "Carnegie Halls" as it consists of three concert venues: the Isaac Stern Auditorium (2,800 seats), the Joan and Sanford I. Weill Recital Hall (268) and the Judy and Arthur Zankel Hall (599).

For many years, Carnegie Hall (below, the entrance area, and left, the Isaac Stern Auditorium) was home to the New York Philharmonic under conductors such as Arturo Toscanini, Bruno Walter and Leonard Bernstein. When the Philharmonic moved to Lincoln Center, Carnegie Hall faced demolition that was averted after spirited protest. It's a good thing, too. Everybody who is anybody would love to perform here.

COLUMBUS CIRCLE, TIME WARNER CENTER

Midtown's north-western tip is formed by Columbus Circle, the gateway to the Upper West Side. In the middle of the roundabout there is a statue of Chrisopher Columbus by Gaetano Russo that was erected in 1892 to commemorate the 400th anniversary of the "discovery" of America. The statue is also the reference point for measuring distances to and from the city as well as a major landmark and point of attraction. It is also a good place to arrange to meet people. The angular glass edifice of the Time Warner Center, built in 2004 based on a design by architect David Childs, continues the traditions of the twin towers built on the west side of Central Park. Situated inside the complex, which cost $1.8 billion, are the headquarters of Time Warner Inc., CNN's studios, luxury apartments, a Mandarin Oriental Hotel as well as several restaurants, stores and a wholefood market.

Columbus doesn't bat an eyelid, no matter how hectic the traffic around him is. No wonder; he is made of marble (a present from the Italian-Americans to the city). The square is dominated by the two 229-m-high (755-ft) towers (bottom and far left) of the Time Warner Center. Several of its floors are dedicated to shopping including the shops at Columbus Circle (left).

CENTRAL PARK UND UPPER EAST SIDE

North of 59th Street, Central Park divides Manhattan into the Upper East Side and the Upper West Side. The park is a green oasis in the center of the urban mass, and people who live near it can count their blessings: a view that looks out over some form of green space rather than other buildings has become virtually unaffordable in New York. Madonna's own townhouse on the Upper East Side is said to have changed hands for a cool $40 million. Running along the eastern edge of Central Park, Fifth Avenue turns into "Museum Mile" with some of the best museums in the city.

A big rectangle cut into the urban jungle, the true dimensions of Central Park only become apparent when viewed from above. The Upper East Side (in the foreground) was once known as the "Silk Stocking District".

BLOOMINGDALE'S

Before dedicating yourself to the sublime, the beautiful and the true, you may be tempted by more decadent goods at Bloomingdale's further east on the Upper East Side. By 1930, an entire block between East 59th and 60th Streets and Lexington and Third Avenue had been transformed into a temple of consumption designed by architects Starrett & Van Vleck. You can browse and shop to your heart's content here, whether for furniture, clothing or household goods, and only the best is stocked in the New York headquarters of this department store chain founded in 1860 by two brothers named Joseph and Lyman Bloomingdale. The prices are often even lower than one might expect. Fashionable shoes, fabulous handbags, designer clothes, you name it, and when there is so much on offer, decisions get tough. Spending money becomes an art form.

The shop window displays at Bloomingdale's have become legendary in their own right. They are rearranged on a frequent basis throughout the whole year, and not just in the run-up to Christmas. In addition to showcasing the rich variety of goods on offer, they highlight the ingenuity of the window display designers. Many a store owner comes from afar to seek inspiration here.

STRAWBERRY FIELDS FOREVER: JOHN LENNON'S DREAM

Everybody has a dream. But only some are able to use their dreams to touch the hearts of others. When John Lennon (1940-1980) sang "Imagine," the world held its breath. That was in 1971, by which time the Liverpool-born John Winston Lennon (who owed his second given name to his mother's brief dalliance with patriotism) had been through both heaven and hell. Born during an air raid, he had experienced great misfortune early in life, having gone to live with his aunt and uncle at the age of two; his mother was run over by a car, and his uncle died of a hemorrhage. It is possible that John experienced life as a fantastic journey not unlike that described in his beloved 'Alice in Wonderland': from meeting Paul McCartney, who was two years younger than himself, to the overwhelming success of The Beatles; from his first marriage to Cynthia Powell to his second with Yoko Ono; from the breakup of the Beatles to creative crises and new artistic challenges. John Lennon had seen and experienced just about everything a person can see and experience by the time he moved into his last home in New York's Dakota Building on Central Park. He still had a dream then, a dream that was perhaps greater than he was himself but which cannot be destroyed: "Imagine."

On December 8, 1980, John Lennon was shot in front of the Dakota Building in New York by a mentally deranged assassin. Yoko Ono commissioned a small garden in his memory in Central Park and named it after a song by her husband: *Strawberry Fields*. It was also the name of an orphanage, run by the Salvation Army in Liverpool near to where John Lennon had grown up.

CENTRAL PARK

Construction began on Central Park in north Manhattan in 1858. It was the realization of a lifelong dream for American landscape architect Frederick Law Olmsted and his partner, British-born Calvert Vaux. Together they created a "green lung" in the ever-expanding city that extends from 59th to 110th Street and covers a vast 340 ha (1,016 acres). It makes up six percent of Manhattan's total area and became the second-largest park in the city after Jamaica Bay Park in Queens (1,150 ha/3,440 acres). Free open-air concerts are held here in the summer. For more information go to the Visitors' Center located in a neo-Gothic building designed by Olmsted and Vaux called the Dairy. The park also contains a zoo, a large lake called the Reservoir (between 71st and 78th streets) where row boats can be hired, and Belvedere Castle where you can enjoy panoramic views over the park.

Nothing about the artificially landscaped Central Park is natural, but it sure makes a naturally beautiful impression. Many millions of cartloads of soil and stones had to be hauled to this site, and more than 500,000 trees and shrubs had to be planted to turn what was a swampy area into a delightful recreation area. On Sundays in particular, Central Park turns into an open-air stage for the city's inhabitants.

METROPOLITAN MUSEUM OF ART

Along with the British Museum in London, the Louvre in Paris, and the Hermitage in St Petersburg, the Metropolitan Museum of Modern Art, known as the "Met" for short, is one of the greatest art museums in the world. Designed by Calvert Vaux and Jacob Wrey Mould, the structure has been expanded several times since its construction in 1870, and houses more than two million exhibits from five thousand years of art history. Founded by wealthy New Yorkers and leading artists of the day, the Met is intended to make art accessible to the people. First-time visitors are overwhelmed by the sheer scope – where else can you see an Egyptian temple, a Rembrandt self-portrait and Frank Lloyd Wright's studio under the same roof? And speaking of roofs...Along with other highlights, the Met has a sculpture garden on its roof terrace with a fantastic view of Central Park and the Manhattan skyline.

The museum receives more than five million visitors each year and it does not always seem to be just about the art here. At the opening of the new American wing in May 2009, Michelle Obama, the First Lady, revealed that the museum had been the location of her first date with her husband: "... and it was obviously wonderful. It worked!"

FRICK COLLECTION

In 1905, Pittsburgh steel magnate Henry Clay Frick (1849–1919) and his wife moved to New York to live out their twilight years. An avid art collector, Frick built an imposing French neoclassical townhouse for $5 million on the corner of Fifth Avenue and 70th Street. It was designed by Carrère & Hastings and was to become a very worthy setting for his great collection. Frick later bequeathed the house, which covers a full city block, and its valuable contents to the nation in 1935. After the death of his wife, Adelaide Frick, it was turned into a museum that is now one of the best in the country for it size. It houses a collection of Old Masters as well as French furniture, enamelwork from Limoges, Italian Renaissance bronzes, and oriental carpets. Highlights include Holbein the Younger's beautiful *Portrait of Sir Thomas More* and *The Polish Rider* by Rembrandt.

When Henry Clay Frick saw the "Millionaires' Row" residence of his arch rival Andrew Carnegie, he decided to build a villa so pompous that it would "make Andy's place look like a miner's shack" (right). It still features a church organ on the staircase (far left). Among the exhibition's treasures (below left) are works by Jean-Honoré Fragonard (left) and Georges de La Tour (below).

WHITNEY MUSEUM OF AMERICAN ART

In 1918, Gertrude Vanderbilt Whitney (1875–1942), who was a respected sculptor in her own right, opened an art gallery in her studio in Greenwich Village. She concentrated on American contemporary art and by the end of the 1920s had amassed a collection of about 700 canvases and sculptures that she intended to donate to the Met. Her gift was refused, however, because the museum was more interested in European art. As a result, she founded the Whitney Museum of American Art in 1931, and it is now considered one of the most significant collections of 20th and 21st-century American art. All the big names including Edward Hopper, Jasper Johns, Roy Lichtenstein and Andy Warhol are represented here. Today, the Whitney makes a point of exhibiting living artists and its annual and biannual exhibitions are known for displaying the work of lesser known artists.

To this day, there is a sense of obligation to honor its founder's dedication to nurturing contemporary American art. This takes the form of solo shows (below left and right, works by Sol LeWitt) as well as the Whitney Biennial of American Art, which first took place in 1932. Built based on plans by Bauhaus student Marcel Breuer in 1966, the museum building (left) is intended to recall an inverted pyramid.

SOLOMON R. GUGGENHEIM MUSEUM

Neither Frank Lloyd Wright, the architect who designed the museum's original building as his last major work, nor Solomon R. Guggenheim, the coal and steel industrialist who commissioned it, lived to see this iconic building's inauguration in 1959. They were thus spared the initially scathing criticism the museum attracted. John Canaday, art critic of the New York Times, is recorded as saying: "The Solomon R. Guggenheim Museum is a war between architecture and painting in which both come out badly maimed". Resembling an inverted snail shell from the outside, the building took sixteen years to complete and is lit from above by a glass skylight. A central spiral ramp runs through the interior from the main level to the top of the structure. The Guggenheim houses an internationally renowned collection of impressionist, post-impressionist and contemporary art.

Frank Lloyd Wright's museum building for the collection of millionaire Solomon R. Guggenheim is as impressive on the inside as it is on the outside. The interior features a ramp winding around the 28.5-m-high (83-ft) rotunda five times at a five percent grade. It houses one of the largest collections of Kandinsky paintings as well as works by Chagall, Feininger, Manet, Marc, Miró, Mondrian, Picasso and Renoir.

EAST HARLEM – "EL BARRIO"

Known as "Spanish Harlem" or simply "El Barrio" (Spanish for "neighborhood"), this famous area east of Fifth Avenue between 96th and 125th Streets is home to the largest Latino community in New York. It consists mainly of Puerto Ricans but there are many Dominicans, Cubans and Mexicans as well. In the 1960s and 1970s, East Harlem was one of the poorest parts of New York and even today the difference between this part of the city and the smart Upper East Side is unmistakable. Conditions have improved markedly, nonetheless, and Latinos are rightly proud of their neighborhood, which has brought forth musicians such as Ray Barretto, Eddie Palmieri and Tito Puente. Mount Sinai Hospital is considered one of the finest in the United States, Latino art and culture is on display at the Museo del Barrio, and no street parades are more exuberant than the ones held here.

American Graffiti goes Muralismo: In view of the cultural background of many East Harlem immigrants, it is not surprising that some of the murals in this part of town are reminiscent of the Mexican murals of, say, Diego Rivera (below). Left: El Museo del Barrio was established in East Harlem in 1969 by a group of Puerto Rican artists and artists of African origin centered around Raphael Montañez Ortiz.

EAST SIDE STORY: HISPANICS IN NEW YORK

Leonard Bernstein's musical *West Side Story* was originally supposed to be called *East Side Story*. In fact, the original version of the musical as it was first performed on September 26, 1957 in New York was called *East Side Story*. Choreographer Jerome Robbins came up with the idea. The rival gangs in the musical take their inspiration from Shakespeare's *Romeo and Juliet* and were at first going to be separated by their religious backgrounds – Catholic versus Jewish teenagers – but the conflict at the heart of the story was later rewritten as an ethnic one. Since the story was set in New York, it made sense to cast the "Sharks" pitted against the "Jets" as Puerto Ricans, in other words Latinos, or Hispanics, as most citizens of Hispano-American or Spanish extraction have been called by the US government since the 1970s. This term stands in contrast to the Anglos (white people who are not of Hispanic origin). When *West Side Story* was written, roughly four million Hispanics lived in the USA. Today, this section of the population constitutes the largest ethnic minority in the country, counting more than 44 million people (almost fifteen percent of the total population of 299 million). The majority comes from Mexico (64 percent), followed by Puerto Rico (nine percent). Most Hispanics live in New York, now as then.

EAST SIDE STORY: HISPANICS IN NEW YORK

New York's appearance is to a large degree shaped by Hispanics, and not just during the parades, which tend to be particularly colorful and vivacious. In recent years, population growth among Hispanics has been roughly three times that of the population in general. Given that fact, it is perhaps no coincidence that US election campaigners show an increasing amount of interest in them.

UPPER WEST SIDE, HARLEM AND NORTHERN MANHATTAN

Bound by Central Park, the Hudson River, 59th and 125th Streets, the Upper West Side is also an affluent area like its counterpart on the East Side. The adjacent district of Morningside Heights is home to churches, colleges and other institutions such as the Jewish Seminary of America, Columbia University (known as the "Acropolis of the academic world"), and the still unfinished Cathedral of Saint John the Divine. Named after Haarlem in Holland and originally a Dutch settlement, Harlem is today a bastion of black culture and has undergone some rapid gentrification since the 1990s.

There are some very exclusive residential blocks on the park including the two imposing towers of Majestic Apartments (far left in the picture) and the San Remo Apartments (below). Between them are two smaller but no less elegant neighbors, the Dakota and the Langham buildings.

LINCOLN CENTER FOR THE PERFORMING ARTS

Situated on Columbus and Amsterdam Avenues between 62nd and 66th Streets, the Lincoln Center for the Performing Arts is a cultural complex that includes the Metropolitan Opera, the New York City Ballet and the New York Philharmonic Orchestra. Planned on the initiative of a group of civic leaders, among them John D. Rockefeller III, most of the complex was built in the 1960s under the direction of architect Wallace K. Harrison. Rockefeller was a major fundraiser and made a significant contribution from his own funds. The chosen site was a former slum area called "San Juan Hill", the scene of fights between rival street gangs that inspired Leonard Bernstein to write the musical *West Side Story*, filmed in 1961. The complex forms part of the comprehensive series of renovations that was designed to improve conditions in this otherwise infamous part of the Upper West Side.

The Metropolitan Opera House (left, showing the fountain illuminated at night on Josie Robertson Plaza) is the heart of the cultural center. It is flanked by the David H. Koch Theater (left side of main picture) and the Avery Fisher Hall (right side of main picture) of the New York Philharmonic. All of these buildings were made of Italian travertine, a light-colored stone used for construction and decoration (calcareous tuff).

METROPOLITAN OPERA HOUSE

The "Met" is one of the world's greatest opera houses – singing here is like qualifying for the equivalent of the opera Olympics. The façade of the house, built in 1966 and designed by Wallace K. Harrison, also has an Olympian feel. Five strikingly high arched windows allow a view into the foyer where two murals by Marc Chagall, both some 10 m (33 ft) square, proclaim the origins and triumphs of music. With an estimated value of $20 million, these paintings are not only objects of beauty but also collateral for a loan that the Met was forced to take out in the spring of 2009 as a result of the global credit crunch. Luciano Pavarotti achieved world fame here, and Plácido Domingo is a regular member of the Met's roster. The original opera house, the Old Met, where Caruso and Callas once sang, was on Broadway. It opened in 1883 with a performance of Faust, but was demolished in 1967.

There are 3,800 seats at the Met (far left) for those who want to attend opera performances such as Wagner's *Rheingold* (bottom left), those who would like to pay homage to stars like Plácido Domingo (left), and those who enjoy watching graceful toe dancing (below, a scene from Yuri Grigorovich's magnificent ballet *Spartacus*). Some opera performances are broadcast live to selected cinemas.

BAGEL, BURGER & ZABAR'S: NEW YORK CULINARY DELIGHTS

In the mood for something different? The Wall Street Burger Shoppe will sell you a hamburger for a cool $175. Not a run-of-the-mill burger, of course, but a "Richard Nouveau Burger", named after the mascot of a New York internet site. The tasty snack consists of 280 grams (half a pound) of the finest Kobe steak mince, 25 grams (1 oz) of black truffles, and 60 grams (2.5 oz) of aged Gruyère, topped with a slice of goose liver and a

pinch of gold leaf. This three-star establishment in the Flatiron District has kept ahead of the competition for over fifteen years – in New York almost an eternity. Zagat, a rating agency, has acclaimed it as the "Best Restaurant in New York" four years in a row. Head chef Danny Meyer serves up many surprises with the strangest ingredients. However, New York cuisine is not all bagels and burgers – and Meyer is not the only innovative chef. There is talk

on the Upper West Side of a culinary revolution that began with celebrity chef Tom Valenti, "the flavor king of New York" whose restaurant has been meeting the needs of even the most demanding gourmets since 2001. The best delicatessen in New York and an institution on the Upper West Side, Zabar's has also featured in its fair share of films and TV sitcoms, with mentions in Sex and the City, among others.

BAGEL, BURGER & ZABAR'S: NEW YORK CULINARY DELIGHTS

Bagels – which are only authentic if they have a hole at the center – are true delicacies when served with cream cheese and smoked salmon, but burgers are classic fare in American cuisine. The cheese counter at Zabar's - a legendary delicatessen on the Upper West Side - is a true delight. Everything here tends to be absolutely top quality and you can order online, but that would mean missing out on eating at the counter.

AMERICAN MUSEUM OF NATURAL HISTORY

Founded on 6 April 1869, construction work on the monumental Roman-style building of the American Museum of Natural History began in 1874 based on designs by Calvert Vaux and Jacob Wrey Mould. It was officially opened in 1877 and is the oldest and still one of the largest natural history museums in the world with thirty-five million specimens, only a small percentage of which can be displayed at any one time. The museum comprises fifteen interconnected buildings with exhibition halls and research laboratories offering comprehensive information about the history of our world and cosmos as well as mighty dinosaur skeletons, a life-size replica of a blue whale, and a 19-m (63-ft) Haida Native American canoe made of cedar. The Rose Center for Earth and Space, which also houses the Hayden Planetarium, has extended the exhibition space by a quarter.

The American Museum of Natural History is usually only open during the daytime. What happens on a *Night at the Museum* can be seen in the film of the same name, with Ben Stiller as a night security guard. But displays like the enormous dinosaur skeletons are bound to fascinate during the daytime, too. Another source of inspiration is the 40-m-high (132-ft) Rose Center for Earth and Space (below left).

COLUMBIA UNIVERSITY, CATHEDRAL OF ST JOHN THE DIVINE

Think big... When the Cathedral of St John the Divine on 112th Street is finally completed, it will go down in the history of religious architecture as the largest cathedral in the world. Begun in a Byzantine-Romanesque style by Heins & La Farge, the foundation stone was laid on December 27, 1892, and although a neo-Gothic extension was added by Cram & Ferguson in 1911, the church is still only two-thirds finished. Both construction, and now renovations are an ongoing process. Columbia University was founded in 1754 as King's College and is one of the oldest, largest and, with Harvard, Princeton and Yale, one of the most respected universities in the country – and a member of the Ivy League. Its faculties for law, medicine and journalism are highly renowned and today the university can proudly boast more than fifty Nobel Prize winners amongst its alumni.

COLUMBIA UNIVERSITY, CATHEDRAL OF ST JOHN THE DIVINE

Alma mater, the "nourishing mother", guards the Low Library of Columbia University (left), the main entrance of which is located on 116th Street. The Cathedral of St John the Divine (below) is a monument to the incomplete: construction work on it stopped following the attack on Pearl Harbour in 1941, and did not resume until 1978. In 2001, a fire obstructed progress and the necessary renovations lasted until 2008.

THE CLOISTERS

The Cloisters is a medieval art museum of a kind unique in the United States. Its central building features fragments from cloisters and other medieval buildings that were collected in Europe by sculptor George Gray Barnard and then assembled and expanded into a museum by the architects Allen, Collins & Willis in the 1930s. Thanks to the financial support of John D. Rockefeller Jr, the museum, located high above the Hudson River in Fort Tyron Park in the wooded north of Manhattan, has been a branch of the Metropolitan Museum of Modern Art since 1925. Its collections of medieval art include the *Unicorn Tapestries* – priceless wall-hangings depicting a hunt for a mythical white unicorn that comes back to life when it is killed – and a medieval Book of Hours. The experience is as spiritual as it is historic as you walk through the reconstructed monastic rooms and peaceful chapels.

Testaments to a number of eras were transplanted from one continent to another making it possible to study the medieval architectural history of the 12th to the 15th century at this museum. Displays include fragments of cloisters and chapels (below) and the busts (left) that belong with an altar created in the German state of Baden-Württemberg around 1470.

HARLEM

In 1658 Peter Stuyvesant established a trading post near modern-day 125th Street and named it "Nieuw Haarlem". Mostly German and Irish immigrants first settled here, followed by Italians. It was not until the beginning of the 20th century, when the subway was built, that African-Americans from Lower Manhattan began moving in. More African-Americans from the southern states and the West Indies followed during World War I, and since then Harlem has become the most famous black district in the United States. A focus for the development of an independent black culture, it has also become a byword for the integration problems experienced by the country's various communities, despite being in the "melting pot" of New York. Religion has played an important role in Harlem's community – there are over 400 churches of many different denominations and several mosques.

After the Wall Street Crash of 1929, Harlem degenerated into a slum. It was not until the 1980s that a development dubbed the "Harlem Renaissance" began to take place. Nowadays, this neighborhood is anything but a slum. Even Bill Clinton – who was described as "America's first black president" by the African-American Nobel-Prize laureate (for literature) Toni Morrison – now has an office here.

ABYSSINIAN BAPTIST CHURCH

In the past, the Abyssinian Baptist Church was home to the biggest Protestant community in the USA, with a history going back to 1808, when black members of the congregation of the First Baptist Church in the City of New York left because it had a segregated area for people of color. In 1923, Adam Clayton Powell, the first pastor, and his congregation moved into the new church on what was then West 138th Street. Powell ultimately drew thousands of black people to Harlem and preached a social gospel that combined spirituality with social engagement. His son, Adam Clayton Powell Jr was also a pastor and avid civil rights activist, and later became the first black person to be elected to Congress, where he was one of the representatives for New York. The name of the church is based on an old name for Ethiopia as this was the country of origin of members of the church's original congregation.

Built according to plans by Charles W. Bolton & Sons and completed in 1923, the Abyssinian Baptist Church (left) is located between Malcolm X Boulevard and Adam Clayton Powell Jr Boulevard at what is now 132 Odell Clark Place (it used to be called 138th Street). Among Harlem's greatest attractions are the emotive Baptist church services and the rousing gospel choirs that accompany them (below).

HARLEM SHUFFLE: FAITH, HOPE AND JAZZ

Take the "A" Train, once the Duke Ellington Band's signature tune, was an invitation that many people were more than happy to take up – the A line of the New York subway goes from Brooklyn directly to Harlem, right into the jazz-filled heart of the black community. Artists like Sarah Vaughan, James Brown and the Jacksons all got their big breaks here at the legendary Apollo Theater's amateur nights. As the Jazz Museum on East 126th Street points out, no other community has nurtured jazz more faithfully apart from New Orleans. Even today the district is living off the times when the seductive blue notes of jazz would enthral and enslave many a music lover. In her novel *Jazz*, Nobel Prize-winner for Literature Toni Morrison had to resort to drastic measures to end a jazz party: a shot rings out, ending not just the party but also the life of an eighteen-year-old beauty. It soon turns out that love is involved, and jazz of course, the two inextricably entwined. It was also Toni Morrison who described not Barack Obama but saxophone-playing Bill Clinton, who still has an office in Harlem, as "America's first black president", an indication that the holy trinity of faith, hope and jazz is not a question of skin tone. Of Harlem, pianist and composer Willie "The Lion" Smith once said, "I'd rather be a fly on a lamppost in Harlem than a millionaire anywhere else".

In 1939, the saxophonist and native of Kansas City Charlie "Bird" Parker was drawn to New York City where the "Blue Note" jazz label had been founded that same year. Charlie Parker's jazz sessions were to decisively shape the jazz age, and Birdland, the club, was named after him. Other venues for regular jazz concerts are the Lenox Lounge (left) and the many clubs on Sugar Hill (remaining pictures).

125TH STREET

For a long time, Harlem was synonymous with the ghetto, but that isn't the case anymore, especially since even Disney opened a store on 125th Street – the neighborhood's main artery for both traffic and business. Anybody taking the A train to Harlem these days will no longer be met by hostile faces - though some of them may look bored - and some say it has actually become safer than Downtown. The hustle and bustle of 125th Street is not much different from that on 42nd Street in Midtown – the glare of McDonalds and Starbucks lights up intersections and street vendors sell their music. The Hotel Theresa at the corner of 125th Street and 7th Avenue opened its doors in 1913 and though it has long been an office building it is still a memorial of the time Malcolm X met Muhammad Ali here, and Fidel Castro (1960, during a UN session in New York) came face to face with Nikita Khrushchev.

Another of Harlem's main thoroughfares is 125th Street (left), also known as Martin Luther King Jr Boulevard. A statue here reminds passersby of the black member of Congress and active civil rights campaigner Adam Clayton Powell Jr (below left). Those who want to get to know the "real" Harlem should also explore the graffiti-decorated side streets (below) with their hidden clubs, shops, bistros and restaurants.

APOLLO THEATER

The legendary Apollo Theater opened in 1914 on 125th Street in Harlem and was originally called Hurtig and Seamon's Burlesque Theater. At the time, black people were not allowed in, and it wouldn't be until twenty years had passed and several changes of ownership had taken place that African Americans were allowed to watch performances here. The theater ultimately became famous as a result of the Amateur Nights on Wednesdays, which were broadcast live by twenty-three radio stations. Among the stars who emerged from these talent shows was Ella Fitzgerald, who originally wanted to perform as a dancer. Other big names include Billie Holiday, Aretha Franklin, Marvin Gaye and the Jackson Five with Michael Jackson. In the 1960s and 1970s, the venue fell into disrepair until it was bought by the State of New York, declared a national monument and reopened in 1985.

John Lennon knew what he was doing when he said he wanted the very first Beatles concert in New York to be held at the Apollo Theater. Elvis Presley himself may have gained inspiration for his lascivious hip-shaking at the venue. After all, the artists performing here were trendsetters. One of them, Michael Jackson, even became the "King of Pop". Below: A performance by Doug E. Fresh, the "Human Beat Box".

OUTER BOROUGHS

Although it is the most famous of the five boroughs, Manhattan is not all there is to New York. The Bronx, Brooklyn, Queens and Staten Island are all familiar names, but in reality few visitors to New York venture beyond Manhattan. Yes, these boroughs have been noted for their urban decay –, Staten Island is sometimes known as "the forgotten borough" and most people only know Queens from the airport – but slowly things are looking up for the less famous parts of the city. If you have some time to spare, why not venture a little further afield and see for yourself?

Unisphere is the name of the gigantic representation of earth created according to designs by Gilmore David Clarke for the World's Fair of 1964. It has been newly erected near Arthur Ashe Stadium in Queens, named for the first black US Davis Cup team member.

DUMBO

"I wish I had a river / I could skate away on", sings Joni Mitchell in one of her most beautiful songs. The fact that the grande dame of ambitious songwriting immediately thinks of a frozen river on which to skate away points to the fact that she comes from colder climes. She is in fact Canadian. But the weather can turn painfully cold in New York in the winter too, and yet it would be impossible to go ice skating on the East River.

That does not stop romantics from letting their minds soar as Joni Mitchell did, however. The most scenic spot for this is undoubtedly the River Café in Brooklyn. More specifically, it is located in what is now called "DUMBO", or Down under the Manhattan Bridge Overpass, a trendy neighborhood that has developed on what was for many years a disused part of the docklands of Brooklyn.

The comedian Jerry Seinfeld is said to have invented the acronym DUMBO for the area between Brooklyn Bridge and Manhattan Bridge. The River Café – which was first awarded a Michelin star in 2010 – serves seafood accompanied by cozy piano tunes. In 1977, when the restaurant opened, this part of town was not at all hip yet, but the view has always been as beautiful as it is now.

BROOKLYN HEIGHTS

Brooklyn is New York's most populous borough, with some 2.5 million residents. Until the five boroughs were incorporated in 1898, Brooklyn was the fourth-largest city in the United States, and it still has something metropolitan about it: 93 different ethnic groups from 150 countries at the end of the 1990s, with their identities emphasized by enclaves such as Little Odessa and Little Arabia. Brooklyn, originally named Breukelen after the town near Utrecht, began as a Dutch settlement. Brooklyn Heights, an idyllic – and expensive – residential area at the mouth of the East River between the Brooklyn Bridge and the Atlantic River, is now a national monument. The Brooklyn Museum is one of the largest art museums in the country, with exhibits from antiquity to the present day. But history can be found in the streets as well: many are lined with the famous Brownstone row houses.

"I am a patriot," declared Henry Miller, "of the Fourteenth Ward, Brooklyn, where I was raised. The rest of the United States does not exist for me, except as idea, or history or literature." But one does not need to be a local patriot to be excited about this neighborhood, its beautiful brownstones in Brooklyn Heights (left) and the prettiest way to enter Manhattan, over the Brooklyn Bridge. Below: Brooklyn Heights Waterfront.

CONEY ISLAND

Three bridges connect Brooklyn and Manhattan over the East River, their acronym being BMW from north to south: Brooklyn, Manhattan and Williamsburg. Entirely aware of its charms, Brooklyn Bridge, the eldest of the three, delivers the best views including over the Brooklyn Promenade (also known as the Esplanade), which runs along the East River. One of Brooklyn's oldest public attractions, Prospect Park, was laid out in the 1860s by Frederick Law Olmsted and Calvert Vaux who considered it a greater artistic success than Central Park, which they had just completed. It includes a zoo, a wildlife area, a lake and sports areas among its other facilities. The famous Coney Island peninsula in south Brooklyn, with its long beach and fairground, was a major resort in the early 20th century. Today, it has a slightly faded, nostalgic feel, with a hint of salt in the air from the nearby Atlantic.

"Under the boardwalk / Down by the sea /
On a blanket with my baby / That's where I'll
be"– the Drifters once sang in praise of the
seafront of Coney Island, just behind the subway
line. The local amusement park, too, is men-
tioned in the song. Throngs of people enjoy
themselves here during the summer months.
Some even take their iguanas for walks (below
left). Below: the Mermaid Parade.

QUEENS

Covering an area of 313 sq km (120 sq mi), Queens is New York's largest borough. Supposedly more languages are spoken here than anywhere else on earth. About half of the 2.2 million residents are of different ethnic origin, so it seems appropriate that John F. Kennedy International and LaGuardia airports, two of New York's three international hubs, are located in this borough. Resonant names for sports fans include Shea Stadium (home of the New York Mets until April 2009, when the new Citi Field Stadium was opened) and the Arthur Ashe Stadium in Flushing Meadows Park, where the US Open is held. Art fans might be drawn to MoMA's P.S.1 Contemporary Art Center, while the work of Japanese–American artist Isami Noguchi, known for his sculpture as well as classic furniture designs that are still on sale today, is on show at the Isami Noguchi Garden Museum.

It is entirely possible that Queens (below, Arthur Ashe Stadium and French tennis star Gaël Monfils) will become "the next Brooklyn". When rents became astronomical in Manhattan, many people moved to Brooklyn, but the neighborhood became so trendy that the rents there began to rise, too. Both boroughs are on Long Island, a 193-kilometer-long island in the Atlantic that lies parallel to the mainland.

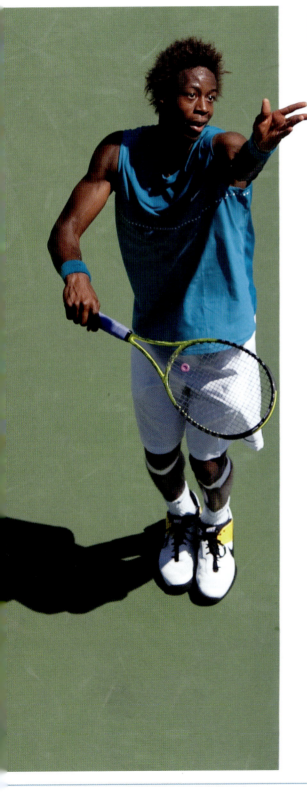

THE BRONX

The only borough of New York to have a definite article and an indefinite future – or so the joke went when the South Bronx ("SoBro") was a byword for urban decay with the highest rates of criminality in the United States. That was in the 1960s, but it had not always been the case. In 1639, when Swedish seafarer Johan Bronck landed on the peninsula that was to be named after him, he felt he had discovered "a land of virgin forest and limitless opportunities". For better or worse, neither have remained the case. People walk with a little more swagger in the Bronx than elsewhere; this is as true of local hip hop heroes as of the heroes in blue and white striped uniforms, the New York Yankees, pride and joy of the Bronx. As in other boroughs, after seeing a decline in the 1970s, there has recently been a good deal of renovation, much of it in the South Bronx.

The restrained charm of sober, no-nonsense architecture (far left, a vehicle depot; below, one of the many indistinguishable basketball courts somewhere in the city) stands in clear contrast to the stadium built for the New York Yankees. Almost a quarter of the local residents, many of whom speak better Spanish than English, come from Puerto Rico; others have emigrated from Eastern Europe and Asia.

HEROES IN PINSTRIPES: THE NEW YORK YANKEES

The New York Yankees are one of the most successful baseball clubs in history. Established in 1901 in Baltimore, Maryland, as the Baltimore Orioles, they moved to New York two years later and went by the name New York Highlanders. They did not become the Yankees until 1913, and now play in the Eastern Division of the American League. With a record of twenty-seven World Series titles they are the most successful professional team in the USA. They can also lay claim to an impressive forty American League pennants. The 'Golden Era' of the Yankees began in 1920, when slugger Babe Ruth joined the team. They ousted the New York Giants to become the city's number one team at the new stadium in the Bronx (the "House that Ruth Built"). When Babe left the Yankees in 1934, another incredibly successful player stepped onto the field, Joe DiMaggio, who was also a darling of the spectators. From then until 1951, the 'Yankee Clipper' (who was to marry Marilyn Monroe after the end of his career) won the championships virtually single-handedly. In the 1960s, the team's performance went downhill and the Yankees missed several playoffs because they did not have replacement superstars. They would not celebrate their glorious comeback until 1998. Since 2009, they have been playing at yet another new Yankee Stadium.

Since 2009, the New York Yankees (from left, Jorge Posada and Alex Rodriguez; below, Derek Jeter) have been playing in a new, $1.5 billion stadium (below left). When dealing with the opposing team, the tone is not always gentlemanly despite their elegant pinstripes. Signs proclaiming "Welcome to the Bronx. Get ready to die!" are no rarity.

BRONX ZOO, NEW YORK BOTANICAL GARDEN

When it was founded in 1899, 843 animals lived in the Bronx Zoo. Today, there are more than 4,000 of them from around 600 different species. The zoo was built on land that had been earmarked for the purpose as early as 1880, in a section of Bronx Park. Just north of the zoo is the New York Botanical Garden. Opened to the public in 1891, its design is based on that of its London counterpart. In the Peggy Rockefeller Rose Garden alone there are 250 varieties of plants. The Enid A. Haupt Conservatory, a Victorian hothouse that contains a tropical rain forest, opened in 1901. The Snuff Mill of 1840 is a reminder of the fact that part of the gardens once belonged to a snuff factory. The snuff producers grew roses with which to perfume their tobacco. The rose garden features more than 2,700 kinds of roses. The Everett Children's Adventure Garden teaches kids about nature in a playful manner.

Bronx Zoo, the biggest city zoo in the United States, is managed by the Wildlife Conservation Society, and covers an area of 107 hectares. Every year, about two million visitors come to see the amazing animals and the fascinating ecosystems (below, the monkey enclosure; left, orchids in bloom at the botanical garden).

A LONG WAY HOME: THE NEW YORK CITY MARATHON

Sharp tongues claim that the best thing to be said about Staten Island – New York's fifth borough – is that you don't have to get off the ferry when it arrives at the terminal and can head straight back to where you came from. On your way there, you will go past Miss Liberty, and you cannot fail to be impressed by Manhattan's glittering skyline. It's possible, of course, that the population of fewer than 500,000 residents on Staten Island sees things slightly differently. The New York landfill site that lies beyond the gates of a community established in 1661 is now closed, but it was once the biggest garbage dump in the world. If that is not a claim to fame! And it is all the more positive if one knows that a park three times the size of Central Park is being built on the old landfill site. In addition, there is a cluster of museums, a bridge and the ferry to Manhattan... Once a year, however - on the first Sunday of November, the world focuses its attention on Staten Island, or at least the part of the world that is interested in running. This is when the New York City Marathon, one of the most important events of the season, takes place. Now officially known as the ING New York City Marathon for sponsorship reasons, it starts on Staten Island but, as is often the case in New York, the final destination of this journey is Manhattan.

The New York City Marathon starts on the Verrazano-Narrows Bridge, which opened in 1964 and is almost 1,300 m (4,290 ft) long. From there, the course leads through all five boroughs. Only 130 runners took part in the first marathon, which took place in Central Park, and only fifty-five of them arrived at the finishing line. It is so popular now, though, that the number of participants has had to be limited to 37,000.

INDEX

A

Abyssinian Baptist Church 228-229
Adams, John Quincy 35
Aguilera, Christina 167
Alexander Hamilton US Custom House 26-27
Ali, Muhammad 112, 232
Allen, Woody 126
Alphabet City 77
American Museum of Natural History 220-221
Apollo Theater 230, 234-235
Art Déco 99, 115, 128-129, 136, 164-165
Arthur Ashe Stadium 237, 244-245
Astor, John Jacob 136
Astor, William Waldorf 136
Avenue of the Americas (Sixth Avenue) 154-155

B

Ballet Tech 107
Barnard, George Gray 224
Barr, Alfred H. Jr 172-173
Barretto, Ray 208
Bartholdi, Frédéric-Auguste 16
Basquiat, Jean-Michel 81
Battery Park 22-23, 72
Bedloe's Island 16
Berlin, Irving 71
Bernstein, Leonard 168, 185, 210
Bloody Angle 60
Bloomingdale's 170, 190-191
Bogart, Humphrey 93
Bowling Green 33
Broadway 82, 110, 142-145, 155-156
Bronx Zoo 250-251
Brooklyn Botanic Garden 242
Brooklyn Bridge 28, 50-55, 78, 239-242
Brooklyn Heights 240-241
Brown, Henry Kirke 91
Brown, James 230
Bryant Park 120-121, 156
Buddhist Temple of America 60
Burnham, Daniel 96

C

Calvin Klein 156
Carnegie, Andrew 203
Carnegie Hall 184-185
Carpenter, James 175
Carrère & Hastings 79, 120
Cartwright, Alexander 94
Cast Iron Historic District 64
Castle Clinton National Monument 22
Castro, Fidel 232
Cathedral of St John the Divine 222-223
CBS Building 154
Central Park 14, 158, 174, 190, 193-200, 212, 242, 252-253
Chagall, Marc 216
Chaplin, Charlie 126
Chelsea 98-99
Chelsea Hotel 102-103
Cher 89
Childs, David 186
Chinatown 41, 56, 60-61
Christopher Street 37, 88

Christopher Street Day 88
Chrysler, Walter P. 124
Chrysler Building 110-111, 116, 124-125
Citygroup Center 140-141
City Hall 56
City Hall Park 48, 56
Civic Center 56-57
Clarke, Gilmore David 237
Clinton, Bill 227, 230
Clock Tower Building 55
Cloisters 212, 224-225
Cohen, Aviad 72
Coltrane, John 76
Columbia University 222-223
Columbus Circle 186-187
Comden, Betty 168
Condylis, Costas 133
Coney Island 152, 242-243

D

Dakota Building 192-193, 213
David H. Koch Theater 215
Davis, Bette 99
DiModica, Arturo 33
Dinkeloo, John 24
Domingo, Plácido 217
Donna Karan 156
DUMBO 79, 238-239

E

East River 28-29, 50, 56, 238, 240, 242
East Side Tenement Museum 71
East Village 76-77
Eiffel, Gustave 17
Elgin Theater 106
Eliot Feld's Mandance Project 107
Ellis Island 18-19, 22
Empire State Building 110-111, 114-115, 125, 163
Everett Children's Adventure Garden 250

F

Federal Hall National Memorial Building 34-35
Federal Style 56
Fifth Avenue 94, 96, 110, 120, 138, 158-159, 170-171, 174-175, 202, 208
Flatiron Building 96-97
Flatiron District 218
Flushing Meadows Park 244
Fort Tyron Park 224
Franklin, Aretha 234
Franklin, Benjamin 48
French, Daniel Chester 27
Fresh, Doug E. 235
Frick, Henry Clay 202-203
Frick Collection 202-203
Fulton, Robert 36
Fulton Market Building 29
Fürstenberg, Diane von 104, 156

G

Garden of Stones 24-25
Gaye, Marvin 234
GE (General Electric) Building 128-129, 160-161, 163, 165

General Assembly Building 130
George Gustav Heye Center 26-27
Ghiberti, Lorenzo 36
Giannini, Frida 175
Gilbert, Cass 26-27, 47
Ginsberg, Allen 76
Giuliani, Rudolph 80, 86
Goldsworthy, Andy 24-25
Goodwin, Philip 172
Graffiti 80-81
Gramercy Park Historic District 92-93
Grand Army Plaza 176-177
Grand Central Terminal 110, 122-123
Green, Adolph 168
Greenwich Village 14, 82-83, 86, 88, 158
Grigorovich, Yuri 217
Ground Zero 42-43
Guggenheim, Salomon R. 206-207

H

Hale, Nathan 57
Hambleton, Richard 81
Hamilton, Alexander 26-27, 30
Handwerker, Nathan 152
Hardenbergh, Henry J. 176
Haring, Keith 76, 81
Harlem River 78, 158
Harrison, George 112
Harrison, Wallace K. 214, 216
Heye, George Gustav 26
Heyl, Charline von 100-101
High Bridge 78
High Line Park 108-109
Holiday, Billie 234
Holocaust, A Living Memorial to the 24-25
Hoover, Herbert 114
Hopper, Edward 204
Hudson River 14, 38-39, 82, 98, 212, 224
Hunt, Richard Morris 200

I

Isamu Noguchi Garden Museum 244

J

Jackson Brothers/Jackson Five 230, 234
Jackson, Michael 234-235
Jamaica Bay Park 194
James, Henry 82
Jewish Plymouth Rock, The 72
Johns, Jasper 204
Josie Robertson Plaza 215
Joyce Theater 106-107

K

Katz's Delicatessen 74-75
Kerouac, Jack 76, 127
Kesselman, Jonathan 72
Kevin Wynn Collection 107
King's Bridge 78
Koch, Ed 62
Koons, Jeff 76
Kreye, Andrian 178
Krogh, Per 131
Krushchev, Nikita 232

L
Lambert, Eleanor 156
Langham Building 213
Lawrence, Jacob 205
Lefebvre de Laboulaye, Édouard René 16
L'Enfant, Pierre 34
Lennon, John 192-193, 235
Lenox Lounge 231
Lexington Avenue 128-129, 190
Liechtenstein, Roy 204
Lincoln Center 156
Lincoln Center for the Performing Arts 214-215
Lipstick 140-141
Little Italy 61, 66-67
Loren, Sophia 133
Louboutin, Christian 104

M
Macy's 143, 170
Madison Square Garden 112-113
Madison Square Park 94-95
Madonna 167, 188
Mangin, Joseph François 56
Manhattan Bridge 78-79, 242
Marc Jacobs 156
Maridueña, Alan "Ket" 80
Matsuhisa, Nobu 59
McCartney, Paul 192
McComb, John Jr 56
Meatpacking District 104-105
Mercedes-Benz Fashion Week 156
Metropolitan Museum of Art 200-201, 224
Metropolitan Opera House 215-216
Minnelli, Liza 168
Mitchell, Joni 238
Moisseiff, Leon Solomon 79
Moore, Clement Clarke 98
Mohawk Iron Workers 116
Monet, Claude 173
Morgan, John Pierpont 118-119
Morgan Library & Museum 118-119
Morrison, Toni 227, 230
Mould, Jacob Wrey 200, 220
Municipal Building 56-57
Muralismo 81
Museum of Jewish Heritage 24-25
Museum of Modern Art (MoMA) 172-173, 244

N
Newspaper Row 48-49
New York Botanical Garden 250-251
New York City Ballet 214
New York City Marathon 252-253
New York Philharmonic Orchestra 214
New York Public Library 110, 120-121
New York Rangers 112
New York Stock Exchange (NYSE) 30-33
New York Times Building 48
New York Yankees 246-249
"Nine Eleven" 36, 40-41
Niro, Robert de 59, 66, 168
Nixon, Cynthia 84-85
North Cove Yacht Harbour 38

O
Obama, Barack 35, 131, 212, 226, 230
Obama, Michelle 201
Olmsted, Frederick Law 194, 242
125th Street 232-233
Ono, Yoko 192-193
Ortiz, Rafael Montañez 209

P
Palmieri, Eddie 208
Park Avenue 134-135
Parker, Sarah Jessica 84-85
Parson's Dance 107
Peggy Rockefeller Rose Garden 250
Pelli, César 38
Pitt, Brad 81
Plassmann, Ernst 48
Plaza Hotel 176-177
Portman, Natalie 156
Post, George B. 31
Powell, Adam Clayton 228-229, 233
Powell, Cynthia 192
Presley, Elvis 235
Puente, Tito 208
Pulitzer Fountain 176

Q
Queens 194, 236-237, 244-245

R
Radio City Music Hall 165-166
Ralph Lauren 156
Reed, John 82
Ringling Brothers and Barnum & Bailey Circus 112
River Café 238-239
Rivera, Diego 209
Robbins, Jerome 210
Robert F. Wagner Jr Park 22-23
Robert M. Morgenthau Wing 24
Roche, Kevin 24
Rockefeller, John D., Jr 130, 172, 224
Rockefeller Center 128-129, 160-163, 165
Roebling, John August 50
Root, John Wellborn 96
Rose Center for Earth and Space 220-221
Rothafel, Samuel 166
Rugglers, Samuel B. 92

S
St Bartholomew's Church 128
St Patrick's Cathedral 138-139
St Paul's Chapel 44-45
San Gennaro Festival 68-69
Scorsese, Martin 66, 126, 168
Seton, Elizabeth Ann 138
Sevingny, Chloë 156
Sex and the City 84-85
Shea Stadium 244
Sherman, William Tecumseh 176-177
Sinatra, Frank 168-169
Sixth Avenue 86, 98, 154-155
Smith, Patti 102-103
SoHo 14, 62-63, 65, 170

Solomon R. Guggenheim Museum 206-207
Sony Tower 140-141
South Street Seaport Historic District 28-29
Spears, Britney 167
Staten Island Ferry 20-21
Statue of Liberty 16-17, 21-22, 252
Stone, Edward Durell 172
Stuyvesant, Peter 226

T
Tamango's Urban Tap 107
Taniguchi, Yoshio 172
The Bronx 29, 66, 236, 246-247
Times Square 110, 142, 146-151
Time Warner Center 186-187
Tobin, Steve 36, 44
Toscanini, Arturo 185
TriBeCa 58-59, 170
Trinity Church 36-37
Trump, Donald 132, 174
Trump Tower 110, 174-175
Trump World Tower 132-133
Tuthill, William B. 184
Twin Towers 42

U
Union Square 90-91
United Nations Headquarters 130-131
Upjohn, Richard 36

V
Vanderbilt, Cornelius 122
Vaughan, Sarah 230
Vaux, Calvert 194, 200, 220, 242
Verrazano, Giovanni da 23
Verrazano Narrows Bridge 253
Village Halloween Parade 86-87

W
Waldorf-Astoria Hotel 136-137
Wall Street 30-33
Walter, Bruno 185
Warhol, Andy 90, 100, 173, 204
Washington, George 31, 35, 83, 91
Whitney, Gertrude Vanderbilt 204
Whitney Museum of American Art 204-205
Williamsburg Bridge 78, 242
Woolworth, Franklin Winfield 46
Woolworth Building 46-47
World Financial Center (WFC) 22, 38-39
World Trade Center Site (Ground Zero) 39, 40, 42-43, 45, 114
Wright, Frank Lloyd 200, 206-207

Z
Zabar's 218-219

PICTURE CREDITS / IMPRINT

Abbreviations:
A = Alamy, C = Corbis, G = Getty, L = Laif, M = Mauritius

Cover and p. 1 Premium/Stock Images/Harris, 2/3 H. & D. Zielske, 4/5 H. & D. Zielske, 6/7 H. & D. Zielske, 8/9 G/Digital Vision/Martin Child, 10/11 G/Flickr/Enzo Figueres, 12/13 G/Stone/Kirk Edwards, 14/15 G/National Geographic/M. Yamashita, 16/17 L/Peter Gebhard, 17l G/Comstock Images, 17r G/Flickr/ Philippe Sainte-Laudy Photography, 18t L/Heeb, 18b C/Visions of America/Joseph Sohm, 18/19 C/Bob Krist, 19l C/Underwood & Underwood, 19r C/Bettmann, 20/21 Christian Heeb, 20l Christian Heeb, 22/23 C/Michael Yamashita, 23 G/Panoramic Images, 24/25 A/Jeff Greenberg, 25 A/Tim Wright, 26 A/Nikreates, 26/27 Martin Sasse, 27l A/M. Flynn, 27r C/Gail Mooney, 28/29 C/Rudy Sulgan, 29 C/Robert Harding World Imagery, 30/31 H. & D. Zielske, 31 G/Panoramic Images, 32/33 C/Creasource, 33l L/Tatlow, 33r L/Volz, 34/35 Bildagentur Huber, 35l G/Spencer Platt, 35r C/Pool/Daniel Acker, 36/37 M/CuboImages, 37 Martin Sasse, 38/39 A/Mathias Beinling, 39 LOOK/Franz Marc Frei, 40, C/Ocean, 40/41 C/Richard H. Cohen, 41 G/National Geographic/Ira Block, 42/43 L/Polaris/Allan Tannenbaum, 43l G/Digital Vision/Lou Jawitz, 43r C/Andrew Holbrooke, 44 M/A, 44/45 Lokomotiv/Thomas Willemsen, 45l G/Mario Tama, 45r L/S. Falke, 46/47 L/Sasse, 47t G/Photodisc/Donovan Reese, 47r M/A, 48/49 M/A, 49tl A/Mary Evans Picture Library, 49tr A/North Wind Picture Archives, 49r Martin Sasse, 50t L/hemis, 50b Martin Sasse, 51-54 C/Richard Berenholtz, 55t Huber/G. Simeone, 55b G/Flickr/Rick Elkins, 56/57 G/Stone/Frank Schwere, 57 M/A, 58 F1online/Tom Hoenig, 58/59 Martin Sasse, 59 M/A, 60, Martin Sasse, 60/61 C/Bob Krist, 61 G/Axiom Photographic Agency/Marc Jackson, 62/63 Christian Heeb, 63tl L/Redux/New York Times, 63tr L/Redux, 63r Martin Sasse, 64/65 C/Jon Hicks, 65 G/Axiom Photographic Agency/Marc Jackson, 66/67 M/A, 67tl G/Stone/Claire Hayden, 67tr L/Redux/New York Times, 67rt A/Mike Booth, 67rb A/Nic Cleave Photography, 68/69 C/Richard H. Cohen, 69tl C/Richard H. Cohen, 69tr C/Richard H. Cohen, 69r A/dbimages, 70, C/Neville Elder, 70/71 G/Iconica/Diehm, 71tl C/Richard T. Nowitz, 71tr Martin Sasse, 72/73 G/Mario Tama, 73tl L/Jonkmanns, 73tr L/hemis, 73r G/Mario Tama, 74/75 A/Oscar Elias, 75tl avenue images, 75tr LOOK/Engel & Gielen, 76/77 L/Christian Heeb, 77t G/Flickr/William Oberlin Photography, 77rt L/Christian Heeb, 77rb L/Christian Heeb, 78 G/Photographer´s Choice/Mitchell Funk, 78/79 G/The Image Bank/ Jorg Greuel, 79 G/Panoramic Images, 80/81 A/Stacy Walsh Rosenstock, 81tl A/Philip Scalia, 81tr A/Richard Levine, 81r C/Andrew Holbrooke, 82t L/Redux/New York Times, 82b L/Christian Heeb, 82/83 M, 83 G/Panoramic Images, 84/85 A/Richard Levine, 85tl A/Richard Levine, 85tr G/Neilson Barnard, 85r G/WireImage/James Devaney, 86 C/Reuters/

Natalie Behring, 86/87 C/Reuters/Natalie Behring, 87tl L/Christian Heeb, 87tr C/Reuters/Natalie Behring, 88/89 Martin Sasse, 89tl Martin Sasse, 89tr Martin Sasse, 90/91 Schapowlow/Bias, 91tl A/Tomas Abad, 91tr C/Gail Mooney, 91r G/Robert Harding World Imagery/Richard Cummins, 92 C/Hannah Mason, 92/93 L/Redux/New York Times, 93

G/Stone/Jeff Spielman, 94/95 G/Panoramic Images, 95 M/A, 96/97 L/Christian Heeb, 97 G/Flickr/Steve Kelley, 98/99 G/Photographer´s Choice/Maremagnum, 99 M/A, 100/101 Martin Sasse, 101 Martin Sasse, 102t L/Polaris, 102b L/Sasse, 102/103 M/A, 103 L/Polaris/Michael Kamber, 104/105 L/Christian Heeb, 105l M/A, 105r C/Atlantide Phototravel, 106/107 C/Julie Lemberger, 107tl C/Julie Lemberger, 107tr C/Julie Lemberger, 107rt C/Julie Lemberger, 107rb G/Timothy A. Clary, 108/109 L/Stefan Falke, 109tl C/James Leynse, 109tr L/Stefan Falke, 109tr C/David Brabyn, 109br C/David Brabyn, 110/111 Martin Sasse, 112/113 C/Icon SMI/Ben Solomon, 113t C/Reuters/ Brendan McDermid, 113r C/Icon SMI/Anthony J. Causi, 114/115 L/Christian Heeb, 115l Schapowlow/Cora, 115r G/Flickr/Steph Goralnick, 116 C/Bettmann, 116/117 C/Bettmann, 117l C/Bettmann, 117r C/Photo Collection Alexander Alland, 118/119 C/Reuters/Jeff Zelevansky, 119tl L/Redux/ New York Times, 119tr C/Reuters/ Jeff Zelevansky, 119r Bridgemanart, 120/121 C/Reuters/Mike Segar, 121 G/Photodisc/Eduardo Garcia, 122/123 G/The Image Bank/Jorg Greuel, 123tl C/Rudy Sulgan, 123tr G/Photographer´s Choice/Siegfried Layda, 123r Martin Sasse, 124l H. & D. Zielske, 124/125 L/Christian Heeb, 125t L/Peter Gebhard, 126t G/Digital Vision/Martin Child, 126b G/National Geographic/ M. Yamashita, 126/127 G/Flickr/Christian Beierle Gonzalez, 127l G/Flickr/Steve Kelley, 127r G/Photographer´s Choice/Maremagnum, 128/129 L/Christian Heeb, 129t LOOK/age fotostock, 129r L/Christian Heeb, 130/131 C/Brooks Kraft, 131 C, 132/133 G/fotog, 133l L/Multhaupt, 133r L/Multhaupt, 134/135 G/Riser/Michel Setboun, 135l G/Taxi/Toyohiro Yamada, 135r M/A, 136/137 L/Christian Heeb, 137l L/Zuder, 137r A/PCL, 138 C/Richard T. Nowitz, 138/139 M/A, 139 C/Rudy Sulgan, 140, LOOK/age fotostock, 140/141 Martin Sasse, 141 G/National Geographic/M. Yamashita, 142/143 A/Philip Scalia, 143 G/Riser/Mareen Fischinger, 144/145 H. & D. Zielske, 145l L/Polaris/Eirini Vourloumis, 145r L/Redux/New York Times, 146 H. & D. Zielske, 147-150, G/Panoramic Images, 151t H. & D. Zielske, 151b H. & D. Zielske, 152/153 H. & D. Zielske, 153l G/George Rose, 153r G7Flickr/danielkrieger, 154/155 G/Stone/Jerry Driendl, 155 G/Flickr/Donovan Rees, 156l L/Polaris/Jennifer R. Grad, 156 M. L/Polaris/Jennifer R. Grad, 156b L/Polaris/Jennifer R. Grad, 157tl M/A, 157tr L/Polaris/ Andrew Lichtenstein, 157l L/Redux/New York Times, 157 M. L/Redux/New York Times, 157r L/Redux/New York Times, 158/159 L/hemis/Camille Moirenc, 159tl Premium, 159tr C/Rudy Sulgan, 159r L/Christian Heeb, 160/161 Martin Sasse, 161tl G/The Image Bank/Jerry Driendl, 161tr G/Photographer´s Choice/Eduardo Garcia, 161r G/The Image Bank/Gil Azouri, 162/163 A/Peter Carroll, 163l G/Stockbyte/altrendo travel, 163r A/imagebroker, 164/165 M/A, 165t A/Lebrecht Music and Arts Photo Library, 165r M/A, 166/167 H. & D. Zielske, 167t Martin Sasse, 168/169 L/Frank Micelotta, 169tl G/Peter Kramer, 169tr G/Paul Hawthrone, 169r L/Redux/ New York Times, S 170/171 Martin Sasse, 171t G/The Image Bank/Jeremy Walker, 171r Martin Sasse, 172 M/A, 172/173 M/A, 173 G/Mario Tama, 174/175 C/James Leynse, 175tl L/ Stefan Falke, 175tr G/Stone/ Siegfried Layda, 175r M/A, 176 Avenue Images/Index Stock/Lauree Feldman, 176/177 L/ Redux/Mark Peterson, 177 C/Radius Images, 178 L/Christian

Heeb, 179-182 G/Photodisc/Jumper, 183t G/Panoramic Images, 183b G/Photographer´s Choice/Gavin Hellier, 184 G/Stone/Hiroyuki Matsumoto, 184/185 Schapowalow/Heaton, 185 G/Panoramic Images, 186/187 G/Photographer's Choice/ Siegfried Layda, 187l C/Alan Schein Photography, 187r L/hemis/Philippe Renault, 188/189 G/National Geographic/M. Yamashita, 190/191 C/Atlantide Phototravel, 191l C/Radius Images, 191r L/Christian Heeb, 192 G/Chris Hondros, 192/193 C/AFP/Don Emmert, 193 G/Matthew Peyton/Stringer, 194/199 C/Atlantide Phototravel, 195-198 L/Christian Heeb, 199l C/ Radius Images, 199r L/Christian Heeb, 200/201 G/Panoramic Images, 201tl L/hemis, 201tr M/A, 201r G/Stone/Hiroyuki Matsumoto, 202/203 A/Richard Bryant, 203tl Martin Sasse, 203tr C/Geoffrey Clements, 203r C/Francis G. Mayer, 204/205 L/Redux/New York Times, 205t M/A, 205r C/Geoffrey Clements, 206 Martin Sasse, 206/207 Martin Sasse, 207 G/Panoramic Images, 208/209 A/Nikreates, 209l A/Philip Scalia, 209r A/Silvan Wick US, 210, G/Taxi/Erin Patrice O'Brien, 210/211 L/Zuder, 211l C/Catherine Karnow, 211r C/Mark Peterson, 212/213 L/Christian Heeb, 214/215 H. & D. Zielske, 215 G/Photographer's Choice/Hiroyuki Matsumoto, 216/217 L/Redux/New York Times, 217tl L/Redux/New York Times, 217tr L/Redux/New York Times, 217r L/Van Tine Dennis, 218/219 Martin Sasse, 219l Stockfood/Paul Williams, 219r Stockfood/ Eising, 220/221 Bildagentur Huber, 221t Martin Sasse, 221r C/Abraham Nowitz, 222/223 L, 223t Blickwinkel/W. G. Allgoewer, 223 M. C/Reuters/Ray Stubblebine, 233b C/Reuters/ Ray Stubblebine, 224 M/A, 224/225 L/Christian Heeb, 225 C/William Manning, 226 L/Sasse, 226/227 Schapowalow/Atlantide, 227 G/Photodisc/Sami Sarkis, 228/229 M/A, 229 G/New York Daily News Arhcive, 230/231 Martin Sasse, 231tl L/Sasse, 231tr L/Sasse, 231r L/Christian Heeb, 232 L/Contrasto, 232/233 L/Christian Heeb, 233 Martin Sasse, 234/235 G/AFP/Stan Honda, 235t L/Stefan Falke, 235r G/WireImage/Johnny Nunez, 236/237 Martin Sasse, 238/239 C/Andria Patino, 239l C/Andria Patino, 239r L/Bosse, 240/241 G/Photographer's Choice/Murat Taner, 241 M/A, 242/243 Martin Sasse, 243tl C/Aurora Photos/ Kevin Kerr, 243tr C/Bob Krist, 243 M. C/Amy Sussman, 243b C/Amy Sussman, 244 C/Tomasso DeRosa, 244/245 C/PCN/ Paul J. Sutton, 245l Martin Sasse, 245r Martin Sasse, 246/247 C/Alan Schein Photography, 247l Martin Sasse, 247r C/Andrew Lichtenstein, 248/249 C/Tomasso DeRosa, 249tl C, 249tr C/Tomasso DeRosa, 249r C/Tomasso DeRosa, 250/251 G/National Goeographic/Michael Nichols, 251tl C/Photo Images/Lee Snider, 251tr L/Redux/New York Times, 252/253 M/A, 253l C/PCN/Paul J. Sutton, 253r C/PCN/PCN Photography.

MONACO BOOKS is an imprint of Verlag Wolfgang Kunth

© Verlag Wolfgang Kunth GmbH & Co.KG, Munich, 2012

Concept: Wolfgang Kunth

Editing and design: Verlag Wolfgang Kunth GmbH & Co. KG

English translation: José Medina, Jane Michael

Editor: Kevin White for bookwise Medienproduktion GmbH, Munich

For distribution please contact:

Monaco Books
c/o Verlag Wolfgang Kunth, Königinstr.11
80539 München, Germany
Tel: +49 / 89/45 80 20 23
Fax: +49 / 89/ 45 80 20 21
info@kunth-verlag.de

www.monacobooks.com
www.kunth-verlag.de

Printed in Slovakia

ISBN 978-3-89944-617-3

Text: Robert Fischer, Tom Jeier

Translation: All rights reserved. Reproduction, storage on data-processing systems, reproduction in electronic, photomechanical or similar ways only with the express permission of the copyright owners.

All facts have been researched to the best of our knowledge and with the outmost care. The editors and publishers are, however, unable to guarantee the absolute correctness and completeness of the information contained herein. The publisher is always grateful for any information and suggestions for improvement.